M

WITHDRAWN

WITHDRAWN

WITHDRAWN

Gottfried Bammes • The Artist's Guide to Animal Anatomy

Gottfried Bammes

The Artist's Guide
to Animal Anatomy

An illustrated reference to drawing
animals

TRANSEDITION
BOOKS

Printed in 1994 in Spain

ISBN 1 898250 36 7

This edition printed for Bookmart Ltd in 1994

List of contents

Introduction

This book does not start from the outer appearance of the animal body. Instead we start our graphic construction from *within* – an approach that we have tried and tested many times. We first set out the rules in accordance with which the shape of an animal is constructed, rules derived from the animal's environmental adaptation and way of life. This raises the question of the match between the demands made on the animal and its response to them, of functions required and construction able to fulfill those functions. The interaction of these factors makes sense of formal attributes in terms of fitness for purpose. Interdependencies and interactions become clear in details of proportioning, the static and dynamic behavior of the organization of the body as a whole, the details of skeletal construction and the arrangement of its motor forces, the muscles. Students will thus become conversant with criteria that virtually make things fall into place of their own accord, with a little thought; they will learn to see that a form *must be as it is* and *cannot* be any other way.

Learning to understand that forms are governed by *consistent rules* is the gateway to grasping the *essence of form* at all levels of graphic studies. For this study purpose we have selected a small number of representative types of animal form: two herbivores, the horse and the cow, the structural design of which is geared exclusively toward locomotion; as walking and running animals they have attained a high degree of specialization. Next come two carnivores, the dog and the lion, which have undergone modifications in the construction of the skull (in particular the teeth and position of the eyes), the front part of the body (which performs more functions than the rear part), and above all in the extremities of the limbs. Because it is closest to the human form, we only touch on the most universal constructional type, the *anthropoid ape*.

Using these representative examples it is not hard to find similarities with other animal forms. Looking at a *basic structural design* common to all these animal types makes it clear that there is one fundamental form set against which that of an individual species appears as a variant, a special case of the universal. The principle of one structural design with variants is brought home at every turn when we explore proportion. Before embarking on any drawing we learn the characteristic proportions of the perissodactyl (the horse) as opposed to the artiodactyl (the cow), and those of the hunter that pursues its prey (the dog) as against those of the hunter that lies in wait (the cat). The basic principles of drawing set out in Chapter I, and such anatomical knowledge as is here, especially concerning construction, are directly related to questions of proportion. The position in the body of the pivotal points associated with movement is closely linked to proportional attributes. This allows a smooth, logical transition from studies of proportion to studies of resting positions and locomotive movements. Information about the machinery of movement helps make us familiar with the functional system comprising the skeleton structure, the groups of functional muscles attached to it, and their position in relation to the axes of the joints.

This resolves yet another problem: how the muscles work. Moreover, an understanding of how the dimensions of all masses obey consistent rules and of the plastic quality of masses comes automatically with understanding the layout of the muscle system.

Methodical intermeshing of topics also lies behind the learning of particular graphic skills in every chapter. We begin with exercises designed to help toward grasping overall structural plan, continue with studies of proportion and go on to studies of resting positions and movements. At this point, in all chapters, we tackle work going beyond objective study and introduce imaginative drawing. The idea that life studies are an end in themselves would discourage creativity.

However, even a life study from nature should not be thought of as a straightforward reproduction of nature; it should make a convincing statement about the subject and its predominant characteristics. Drawing understood as a constructing process, exploring the interplay of framework forms and variable soft forms, is therefore recommended.

The method of graphic study set out in this book promotes the development of many and varied capabilities and skills: observation, visual memory, powers of visualizing capacity, combinational ability, imaginative power and sensitivity.

Franz Marc, in the words of H. Bünemann, sought 'in all investigative responsibility and seriousness' to capture the structure of the animal organism working 'from its most intractable aspect, the structure of the bones'. He thus accumulated a wealth of inner perception, a sure foundation on the basis of which he was later able to find the large, embracing form and confident, defining line, and even to invent freely imagined fantasy creatures.

It is in this sense that I offer my anatomical approach for artists. Once consistent rules governing form have been recognized, they can be embroidered on. This book sets out to develop the ability to see with understanding and to call on what is known to create a mental image. The visual repertory stored in the artist's head must contain a high degree of practical and visual simplification for only simple things can be remembered.

The working methods outlined in this book, interweaving step-by-step sequences and proposed solutions, are designed to achieve the above goals and tasks in a methodological, systematic program.

We use anatomical analysis not for the sake of analysis, but in order to create order, making connections and discovering consistent rules governing form. An excellent means of doing this is to explore the dialectic between formal and functional connections, to look at the interaction between the demands made on the animal form – as a whole and in its component parts – and its ability to respond to those demands.

I see the transformation of the multiplicity of factual anatomical information into images that can be visualized as one of my most important objectives in teaching.

If the forms that make up the body, the skeletal structure in particular, are to be drawn as distinctive and memorable, this can only be done by seeking for simplicity, reducing forms to elements, distilling them, reaching the essence of form; this is completely different from reproducing their mere outward appearance. Once the key to simplification of form has been found, the door is opened to drawing animal forms from a mental image of them, i.e. without the direct presence of an animal model, to understanding the construction of the body, which is based on the dialogue between the core masses of the body – the thorax, pelvis and skull – and the other constructional framework forms as they interact with the soft, fleshy parts.

Inevitably, not all drawings based on the guidance offered here will be masterpieces, but one thing should give satisfaction to all who follow it: both emotionally and intellectually they will have become close to the creatures with whom we share the earth.

1.

Basic principles in drawing animals

1.1
Deciding on specific impressional qualities

All subjects – here animals – possess their own specific qualities which arouse our interest and invite us to capture them in drawing: these we might call their *impressional qualities*. The student should decide which of the wide range of potential impressional experiences is the most powerful, and start by concentrating only on that, allowing the others to fade into the background. By filtering the way we observe and look at things, we can soon learn what to pick out as essential, which could be any one of a number of things – proportional peculiarities, shapeliness, slimness, delicacy, massiveness, squatness, power, color and structure of skin or coat, actions and functions of the body in repose and in movement. The list could go on and on. Here are some suggestions as to how to select the essential in animal models:

- Go round a zoo, get a general idea of the various forms of animal and make a note of what impresses you most.
- Consider the strongest impression in terms of drawing, not overtaxing yourself by attempting to bring in other attractive aspects, however fascinating they may be.
- Be quite clear as to whether proportion, function, surface texture, solidity or structure excites you most.
- Having reached your decision, concentrate on just that one aspect and attempt to convey it in drawing. If you try to introduce too much into your drawing in one go, there is a risk that no impressional quality will be fully developed – the result will be a jumble of non-essential, haphazard observations with no independent, stable graphic concept.

In capturing the impressional quality we make a first step toward finding *expression*. By proceeding in this selective way we sharpen our perception of formal and impressional characteristics, which *trains us to look for expression as a crucial criterion in every line we draw*. Ultimately this enables us to control a multiplicity of factors and use symbols and shorthand to convey what touches us most.

1.2
Anatomical knowledge used to pinpoint essence

What appears essential to the eye, however, does not depend only on its impressional qualities. Since we must also interpret its substance, we need a basic knowledge of animal anatomy. This enables us to see through the surface of the animal that is the object of our observation and perceive it as an articulated entity (fig. 1), and at the same time prevents it from being dissipated into an accumulation of individually observed details. We need to be able to recognize fundamental factors, not to know all the details of external appearance.

The purpose of anatomical knowledge for artists is to make it possible to construct from within. We deconstruct the superficial visual impact, using anatomical analysis and close observation, in order to reduce things to their essentials and assess main and subsidiary forms.

The artist seeks to use anatomical knowledge to achieve unity and simplicity of form based on insight into essence.

So what are the main points?
- What the *structural designs* of animals have in common and the differences between them. Seeing construction as the body's answer (form) to the demands made on it for performance (function) is crucial in this.
- *Proportional anatomical characteristics* governed by function.
- Following on from the above: establishing *hierarchy of form*.
- *Formal attributes governed by structure and dynamics* (fig. 2).
- How the whole connects.
- Condensing the forms of individual parts of the skeleton (fig. 3) and the joint and muscle systems (figs 86, 88).
- Building up *accurate mental images of form*.
- The structural interplay within the body, helping toward producing a *structural drawing* (figs 11, 130-34).

Seeing the body as a constructed system helps develop a mental reconstruction in which each individual part finds its place in the structural unity of the whole.

This way of thinking quite naturally turns natural appearance into abstract images and makes a statement about animal forms. The artist's own individual way of looking, thinking and behaving will be carried over into artistic activities; this lends attempts to learn and understand about form the necessary stability.

Thus the primary and ultimate contribution of anatomical knowledge for artists as I see it is to make possible a *statement about natural appearance* and to underpin *the power of form to carry conviction*; this contrasts with the essential emptiness of schematic formulas.

1 KNOWLEDGE OF FORMAL
STRUCTURE LEADS TO AN
UNDERSTANDING OF FORM

Anatomical knowledge enables an artist to
see through an organic entity and
perceive it as an articulated unit. This
prevents us from copying outward
appearances slavishly and teaches us
about the structural interplay between
framework forms and the soft parts of the
body.

2 RULES OF FORM BASED ON
DYNAMICS AND STRUCTURE

a) The profile is determined by the
angles of the bones and the muscle
forces that serve to fix the joints in
sequence and so to facilitate locomotive
movement.

b) The back and front views of the
skeletal structure show only slight angles
at the joints. They mainly demonstrate
how weight is transferred onto the feet.
In a simplified linear drawing we see the
course of the statically determined
framework of the rear and front
extremities.

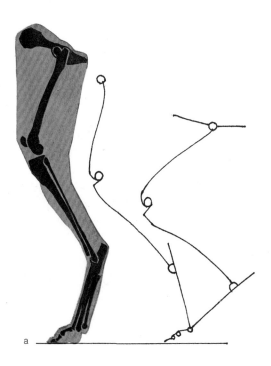

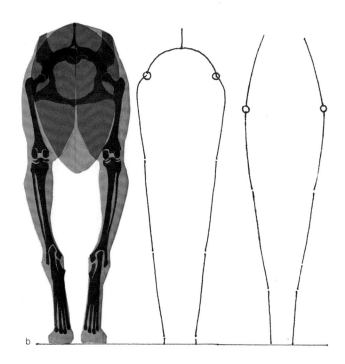

3 ILLUSTRATION OF THE CONSTRUCTION AND SHAPE OF A JOINT

Reducing form to constructional elements produces condensations that are convincingly simple, as in this left hock of a horse; these become concepts that can be conjured up in the mind and put to good use in life studies.

a) The first phase gives the crucial directions and main forms.

b) The second phase shows increasing formal differentiation, emphasizing the unity of form and function. Investigations of this kind reveal recurring sculptural similarities between animals of widely differing forms.

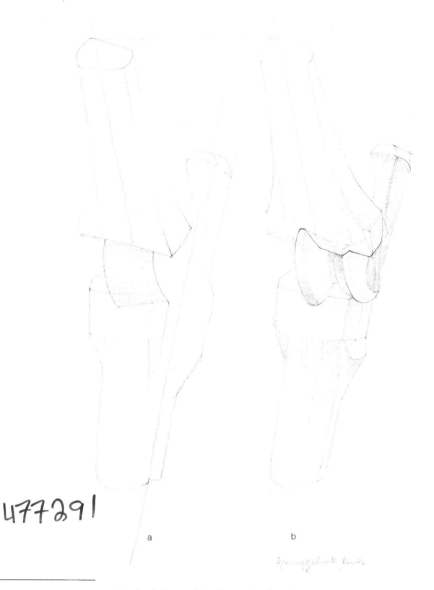

477291

a   b

1.3

Understanding the structural design of an animal

The organic form of an animal represents a system that controls the body and a piece of organization that we describe as a *structural design*. Perceived in this light, it is a working model which makes the main features shared with other forms just as clear as any differences from them.

The body of a mammal is built like a bridge (fig. 4) whose vaulted span is represented by the vertebral column running from the chest to the loins. It is held by two supporting pillars at the front and back, i.e. the front and rear legs, at a height that is specific to the animal in question.

The bridge arch, which is shaped like a flat C, is concave on the side of the animal's abdomen, counteracting the forward and backward thrust exerted by the weight of the trunk. The bridge arch is therefore clamped passively by ligaments in the vertebral column, and actively by the rectus abdominis muscle (fig. 5).

The two forelegs between which the thoracic vertebral column is suspended with the help of flexible straps of muscle (figs 6a, 6b) have to carry the greatest burden, supporting about two-thirds of the total body weight (fig. 4). As a result, between the carpal and fetlock joint it has become perfectly straight (a columnar shape). Non-fatigable tendons and the snap-joint at the elbow (of the horse) provide joint fixings that conserve muscle power (fig. 6b). The slanting direction of the scapula absorbs part of the forward thrust of the vertebral column. *Thus the two forelegs have a primarily supporting function and during locomotive movement they transmit the forward thrust of the trunk.*

The thrust from the *two hindlegs* is transferred without loss of power via the downward-sloping pelvis onto the vertebral column (fig. 7b). Several angles in the skeleton of the leg contribute to this. Straightening out these angles lengthens the limb, so releasing the forward thrust. That is why the two rear legs support only *one* third of the total body weight (fig. 4). The many angles and the particularly powerful extensor muscles of the associated joints are the main factors behind the pushing-off, lifting movement of the hindlegs.

Everything relating to the shape and direction of the bridge structure of the mammal's body, especially the directions followed by the various limbs and their pivotal points (fig. 9), must be thoroughly understood before it can be given elementary graphic expression (fig. 8), because these angles and directions have a considerable impact on the moving thrust.

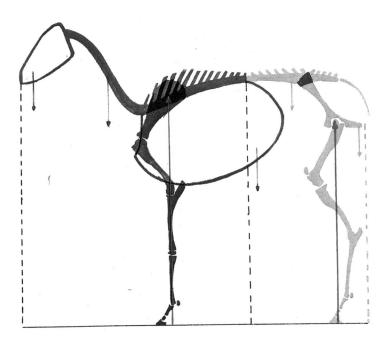

4 PRINCIPLES OF THE CONSTRUCTIONAL DESIGN AND WEIGHT DISTRIBUTION OF THE BODY

The way in which the front extremities have developed into a column and the hind extremities into a push-off force thanks to their extensile joint angles ties in with the fact that two-thirds of the body weight is supported by the front legs and one-third by the rear legs. The red lines indicate the positions of the points of support.

5 THE CRUCIAL SECURING OF THE BRIDGE ARCH

The vertebral column extends like the arch of a bridge between the front and back end of the animal. The pelvis and the shoulder girdle take the thrust (red arrows) developed by the weight of the intestines. The muscles in the hindquarters serve as an anchor for the bridge construction at the rear, and the neck muscles secure it at the front. In brown: bracing by ligaments.

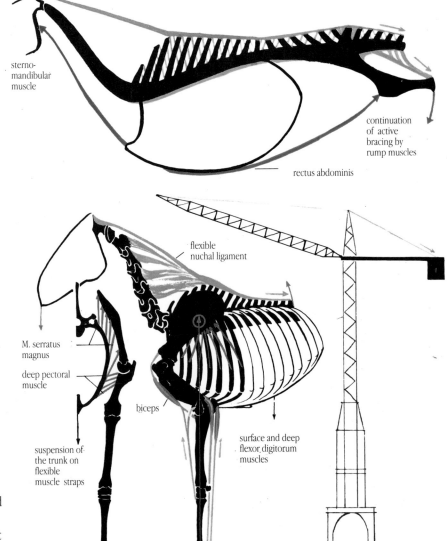

sterno-
mandibular
muscle

continuation
of active
bracing by
rump muscles

rectus abdominis

flexible
nuchal ligament

M. serratus
magnus

deep pectoral
muscle

biceps

suspension of
the trunk on
flexible
muscle straps

surface and deep
flexor digitorum
muscles

a   b

6 CONSTRUCTION OF THE FRONT PILLAR OF THE BRIDGE

a) Front view: suspension of the thorax by straps of flexible muscle between the scapula and the humerus.

b) Side view: joints that carry a particularly heavy load are reinforced by non-fatigable tendons and snap (elbow) joints. The balance between the head and neck on one hand and the thorax on the other is maintained with the pivotal point on the shoulder blade working like the counterweight on a crane.

Section 1.3
Understanding the structural design of an animal

7 CONSTRUCTION OF THE REAR
    PILLAR OF THE BRIDGE

The thrust can be transferred onto the
vertebral column by straightening the
angular joints of the hindleg without any
loss of power because of the position of
the pelvis (slanting downward).
a) The pelvic girdle and leg in back view.
b) The angle of the knee is fixed in
repose by a loop of ligaments and the
other joints by non-fatigable tendons.

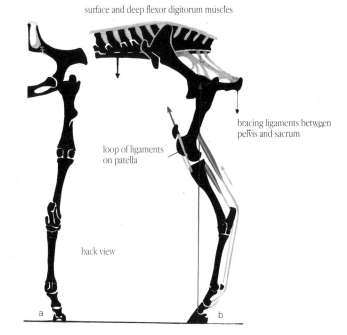

surface and deep flexor digitorum muscles

bracing ligaments between
pelvis and sacrum

loop of ligaments
on patella

back view

a

b

8 STEP-BY-STEP APPROACH TO
    DRAWING THE STRUCTURAL
    DESIGN OF ANIMALS

a) The purpose of the exercise is to make
sure of the directions followed by the
vertebral column and the limbs.
b) The framework can easily be adapted
for movement (study of a cheetah's
movement).

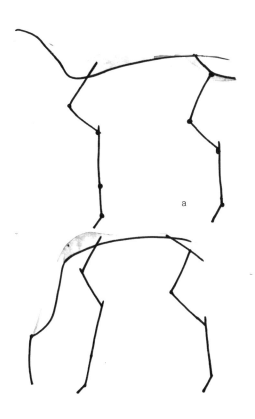

a

b

8c) The behavior of the constructional
framework, the vertebral column in
particular, when upended (large cat).
d) A sitting position and stretching
radically alter the directions studied.

9 MAIN JOINTS AND PIVOTAL POINTS

The horse again serves as a representative
example of how the pivotal points are
situated in the skeletal structure of other
land mammals. The red rings indicate
pivotal points relating to locomotive
movement, the red dots in white rings
other pivotal points.

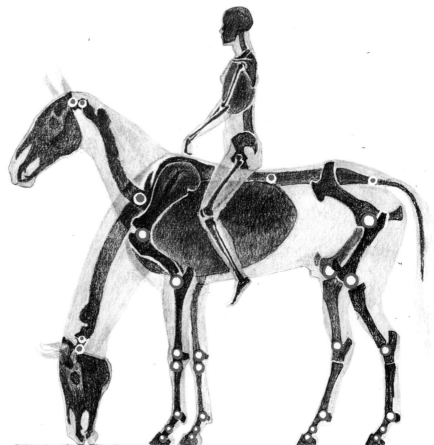

Section 1.3
Understanding the structural design of an animal

1.4

Deciding on a viewing angle

To depict an animal body three-dimensionally it is necessary to be clear about the relationship between the person drawing and the object, the viewing angle and the horizon line, all of which contribute to a perspective view (three-quarter angle, viewed from below or above). Not every viewing angle is equally well suited to displaying distinctive formal features. A direct, unangled view (side, front or back) for example shows fewer of these features than a three-quarter view from above or below (figs 10a, 10b). We also have to consider foreshortening and

intersections (fig. 11). Three-dimensional projections of this kind enhancing distinctive features are essential in depicting animals.

Another factor is important: the position of the body in the surrounding space and its relationship to it. This in turn means making sure that *the body, and all its various sections and parts, has graphically clear viewing planes* enclosing the body with fixed three-dimensional gradients (fig. 11). This requires clarifying the large and small masses and simplifying them, so articulating the spatial gradient of each plane. Drawing in where cross-sections are imagined to be (figs 11a, 11b); helps to highlight the special shape of the body in question.

10 SIMPLIFIED THREE-DIMENSIONAL DRAWINGS HELPING TO JUDGE THE VIEWING ANGLE

The beginner should decide on the horizon line (H, dotted line) or eye level in relation to the animal's body before putting pencil to paper.

a) The horizon line located above the line of the animal's back gives – in addition to the three-quarter angle – a view from above which has the effect of producing a rising line for the standing surface and the general direction of the back line.

b) The horizon line lies through the middle of the body of the animal with the result that all axes above the horizon line fall and all those below it rise.

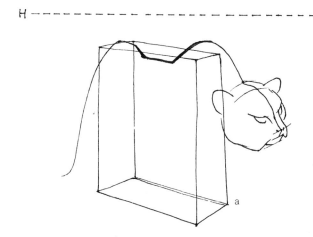

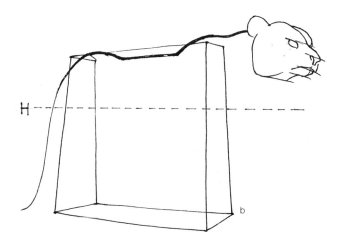

11 USING LINES TO MODEL FORMS AND CREATE CONTRASTS

In using hatching for modeling, the gradients of the planes of the body should be perceived as the meeting of the forms composing it.

a) It is important to express the convergence of planes decisively. Preliminary sketches to clarify things can make the task easier.

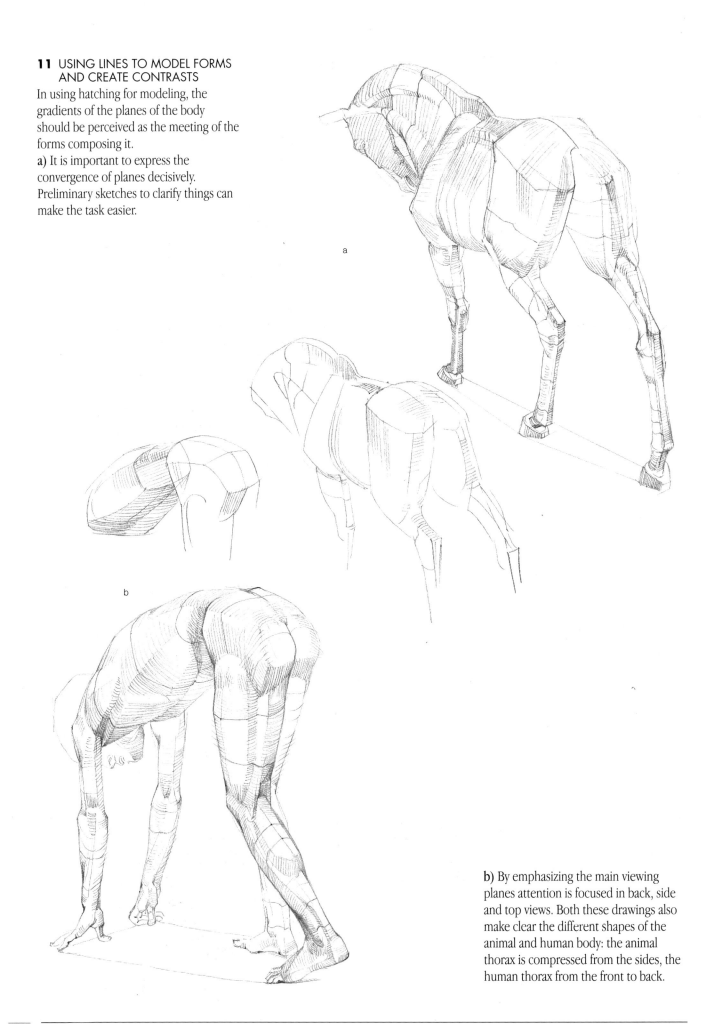

a

b

b) By emphasizing the main viewing planes attention is focused in back, side and top views. Both these drawings also make clear the different shapes of the animal and human body: the animal thorax is compressed from the sides, the human thorax from the front to back.

2.

Body cover textures

As well as proportions, structural and dynamic phenomena and movement, body cover – its coat or the special nature of its skin – is one of the great impressional qualities of an animal's form and appearance. For this very reason it is important that no attempt should be made to imitate its physical appearance. The discovery of graphic techniques that can imply the texture of an animal's body cover is far more effective.

Consideration of this problem now and not later, as a secondary concern, is in line with our intention of broad preparation, laying the foundations of the means to be used to achieve desired effects. The artist needs to build on those graphic expressive possibilities required at the outset. The different body cover textures offer a rich field of activity for conveying distinctive and characteristic features convincingly. Experiment with different techniques is needed.

- Avoid techniques that are remote from nature.
- Every medium has its own expressive language; pencil and pen differ from graphite stick ((fig. 15), red crayon (fig. 16) or chalks, and a brush on a dry ground (figs 14, 22) from one on a wet ground.
- A linear approach with pen and ink will give sharp definition to outlines (fig. 64).
- Inks, conventional or Indian, on a ground sprayed with water (fig. 17) produce fuzzy, exciting textures (figs 142, 143) which it is impossible to control fully.
- Indian ink on an evenly moistened ground (fig. 18) produces clayey, velvety contours.
- Opaque paint, applied half dry with a thick brush, satisfactorily suggests a shaggy, bristly, rough coat (fig. 19). This technique allows rapid, controllable work.
- Using fluid media on grounds of varying wetness means that the colors run, and it is difficult to control their spread. An experienced watercolor artist can exploit this to create a free, airy effect suggesting a fluffy coat (figs 21, 145), but it is impossible to predict technical quirks of this kind reliably or control them fully.
- Effects that are hard to control using mainly marks (fig. 78) contrast with the shapes created using a well-filled watercolor brush (fig. 22). The latter are produced by applying the brush fluently and smoothly, letting it trail, and finally lifting it off the paper.
- A very different method is to use the wax batik process on paper – it can be employed to full advantage in drawings and patterns of the animal body (fig. 20).

12 THE TEXTURAL APPEAL OF
   ANIMAL FUR
Along with renewed interest in natural form there was also an increased awareness of the texture of animal fur in Renaissance art.
Antonio Pisanello (1395-c. 1455), Cheetah, jumping to the right.
Pen and watercolor on parchment,
6¼ x 9 in (16 x 23.1 cm), Paris, Louvre

13 CAPTURING THE FORM OF
   AN INDIVIDUAL SPECIES
This work again shows the artist turning away from the formalistic, medieval approach to the study of animals as an artistic field in its own right.
Antonio Pisanello (1395-c. 1455), Fox, lying down and facing left.
Pen and watercolor on white paper,
5½ x 8½ in (13.7 x 21.4 cm), Paris, Louvre

The way watercolor paint runs when it is freely applied produces lively dappled effects. Furthermore, using watercolor can save a lot of time compared with laboriously drawing in an animal's coat.

The above is by no means an exhaustive list of the basic methods that can be used to convey quite specific body cover textures expressively, and a combination of one or more of these techniques gives a virtually unlimited range. Once a suitable technique has been chosen, avoid doing preliminary sketches which are then worked up in different kinds of materials. They can all too easily disturb or even destroy unity of execution. Sketching constrains and prevents you from setting about finding the best way of conveying surface texture quickly with complete freshness, power and freedom.

Bare skin with no covering of fur or hair also requires us to look for distinctive features. Cracks, armor, bark-like fissures and clusters of wrinkles or scattered creases all have to be conveyed in an individual yet appropriate way.

The recommendations made here and on the following pages are intended as basic guidelines only: there is an enormously rich range of possibilities for conveying textures in a naturalistic way.

14 CONVEYING SURFACE TEXTURE BY MEANS OF COLOR
The horse's short, gleaming coat and its pile are conveyed here by the interplay and modulation of red, pink, carmine, raw sienna, burnt sienna, ocher and olive green.
The author, Mill horse , c. 1950.
Watercolor, $16\frac{1}{2}$x$22\frac{1}{2}$ in (42 x 57.5 cm)

16 THE ELOQUENCE OF RED CHALK
Red chalk or sanguine has similar qualities to graphite. It can be applied on its side or as an edge, delicately touched on or wielded powerfully and incisively. Used with the right paper it can produce very wispy, fluffy effects.
Far right: red chalk applied on its side, its edge and swiveled. These shapes were produced by using the chalk in these different ways <u>without</u> any preliminary sketching.

15 GRAPHITE AND ITS POTENTIAL
Six-sided or four-sided graphite sticks
make an immediate mark – sometimes
too quickly and freely! – producing
marvelously lush lines and emphasizing
painterly effects as well as graphic texture.
Inexperienced users are apt to smudge
their work.

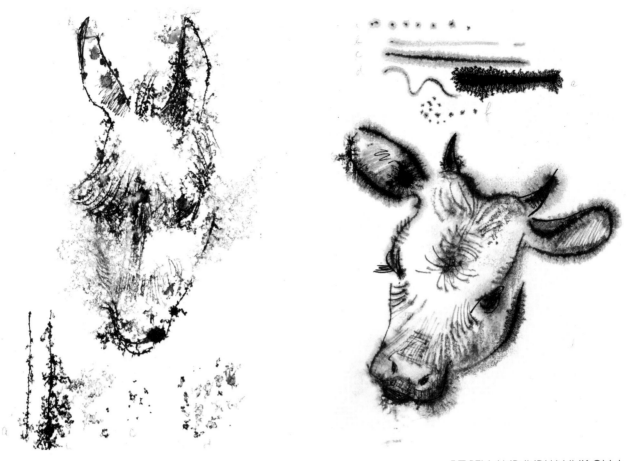

17 PEN AND INDIAN INK ON A
GROUND SPRAYED WITH WATER
When combined with watery substances
Indian ink tends to spread. If you spray
water over paper in a fine mist, the ink
will spread into a network of fine
branches, which can be very helpful in
suggesting a shaggy coat texture.

18 INDIAN INK ON A THOROUGHLY
DAMP GROUND
Indian ink applied to damp fine-grained
watercolor paper tends to run,
producing velvety graphic effects ranging
from light gray to black.

19 GOUACHE PAINT APPLIED
HALF-DRY
Using a free approach and applying
opaque paint with a thick brush,
characteristic coat textures (here the coat
of a Hanuman monkey) can be
suggested. But the drawing must not
turn into a hard-edged silhouette cut-out.

20 BATIK USING A WAX PENCIL ON COLORED PAPER
The batik technique is ideally suited to conveying the markings of an animal's coat. Against a medium-light colored paper the light or white line of the wax crayon stands out particularly well. A watercolor wash is then applied over it, which does not adhere to the wax lines.

21 CREATING TEXTURE BY A PAINTING TECHNIQUE
The running potential that watercolors have when wet is applied to wet has an esthetic appeal all of its own, as well as expressing the soft fluffiness of an animal's appearance.
The author, Angora cat, 1967.
Watercolor, $10\frac{1}{4}$x$7\frac{1}{2}$ in (26 x 18.5 cm)

22 BRUSH DRAWING ON A DRY GROUND

Recording rapid movement from life or from imagination at lightning speed using a well-filled watercolor brush will be expressive only if the brush is smoothly applied and not lifted. The size of the depiction must therefore relate to the size of the brush. Shapes of varying width can be achieved only by varying the pressure used and letting the brush trail.

a) The maximum width of a brush stroke with the brush on its side.
b) A stroke made with the brush full length.
c) A fine line drawn with the same brush.

3.

Learning about proportion – a first priority

3.1

Proportion – a distinctive feature of animal form

The contours given to an animal's form by the proportions typical of its species are at least as fascinating as body cover texture. Animal shapes are rational. Proportion is the expression of an order. We can overlook distinctions such as the difference between a hoof and a paw, but clearly established proportions can virtually stand alone for the unmistakable overall form, in which individual distinctions are then revealed as subordinate. For example, a horse's square proportions are noticeably different from the low rectangle of a cow's body, so much so that there is no need to inspect them more closely and look for the detailed attributes of the perissodactyl or the artiodactyl. Thus studying the proportions of an animal body is a first priority. In depicting an animal body *we must achieve an overriding sense of order, with individual components fitting into a unified whole.* Forming a clear idea of the interrelatedness of the whole comes before any other consideration. This involves:

- Not using a standardized 'basic formula' of the type recommended by many art teachers who force natural form and their students into a set mold.

- Adopting instead a flexible approach which can be applied to any animal type so that every proportional peculiarity can be seen and recognized.

- Avoiding rigid, a priori *rules* of proportion which would be constricting, and concentrate *investigating* proportions.

Proportion may be defined as the relationship of the parts to the whole. The physical structure typical of each species is typified by the interrelationship of its dimensions.

23 PROPORTIONAL
CHARACTERISTICS OF A
HUNTER THAT LIES IN WAIT
(LION)
The relationship between the length
of the trunk and its height from the
ground, expressed as a rectangle using
head length as a module,
demonstrates the low, elongated
proportions of this animal type.

KL = head length

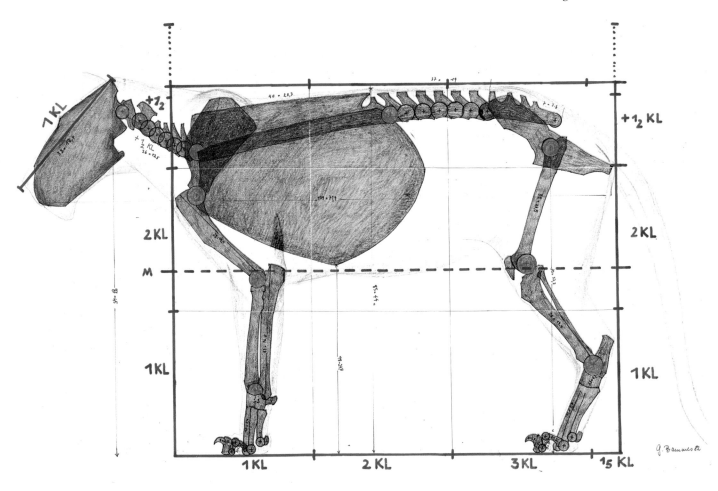

The proportion of the animal tells us something about its way of life and adaptation, and accordingly can be seen as a pattern with a purpose. It conforms to certain rules: for example the proportions of a *hunter that lies in wait* (fig. 23) are different from those of a *hunter that pursues its prey* (fig. 24). Hunters that lie in wait have a squat, massive skeletal structure and musculature, containing an explosive capacity for powerful short-distance sprinting, springing on their prey and bringing it down. Hunters that pursue their prey, on the other hand, keep going until their quarry is exhausted; they are long-distance 'light athletes', needing long legs and a slim, light build.

Animals that lie in wait include the lion, puma, tiger, leopard and panther as well as the short-legged domestic cat. All these species have a low trunk matched by a short, powerful neck and head, whereas hunters that pursue their prey (members of the dog family such as the wolf, coyote, fox and many breeds of pet dog) typically have long legs matched by a long slim neck and head, and large lungs.

Herbivorous running animals (e.g. the horse family) have a trunk that stands high off the ground (fig. 25). Their long legs afford their sole chance of survival when they are pursued. Flight rather than the weaponry provided by offensive tusks or horns

Section 3.1
Proportion – a distinctive feature of animal form

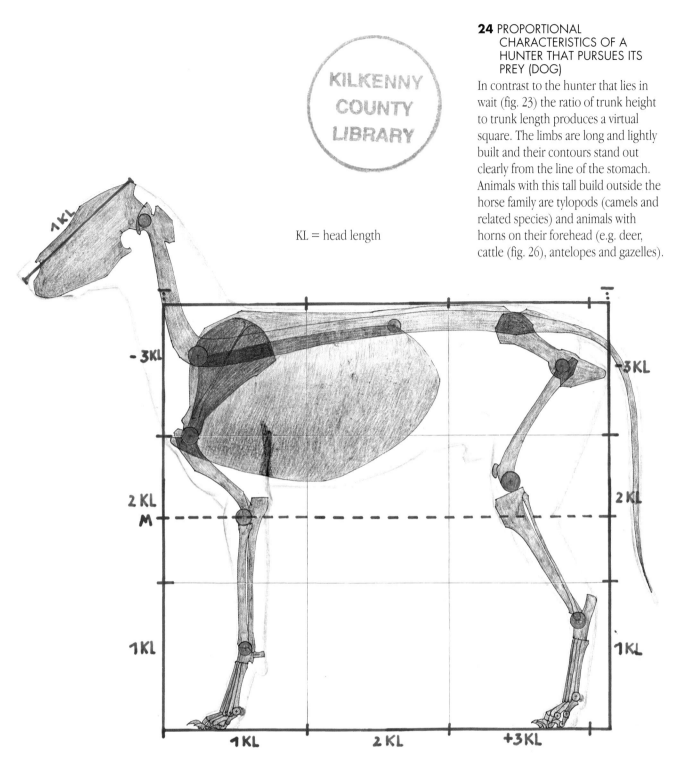

KL = head length

In contrast to the hunter that lies in wait (fig. 23) the ratio of trunk height to trunk length produces a virtual square. The limbs are long and lightly built and their contours stand out clearly from the line of the stomach. Animals with this tall build outside the horse family are tylopods (camels and related species) and animals with horns on their forehead (e.g. deer, cattle (fig. 26), antelopes and gazelles).

for attack and defense is their crucial adaptation to a dangerous environment.

The law of correlation applies again here: as the legs become longer, so does the length of the neck. A short neck suits short legs (ability to reach food).

The proportions of primates differ from those of the animal forms mentioned so far. If the human form is shown on all fours (fig. 27), the torso slopes down toward the head (because of the shortness of the arms) and rises as it approaches the buttocks (because of the length of the legs, shown with a marked bend at the knees in our diagram). The position of the neck end of the

vertebral column and the shape of the head make it hard to look forward. The animal forms mentioned already, however, are perfectly well equipped to look ahead of them.

The anthropoid ape (fig. 28) – a gorilla in our diagram – on the other hand, as a creature that can climb, hang and swing, needs extremely long arms with a long reach. The rest of the body is used as a pendulum. When the gorilla climbs its short legs are used mainly for bracing. The correspondence between way of life and proportion is perfect. The marked difference in the lengths of the front and back legs means that the torso of the primate slopes down steeply.

The height and length of the trunk are those of a square. We perceive such a relationship as harmonious and well balanced. The body is powerfully equipped for running and jumping. The line of the stomach lies at almost half the height of the trunk.

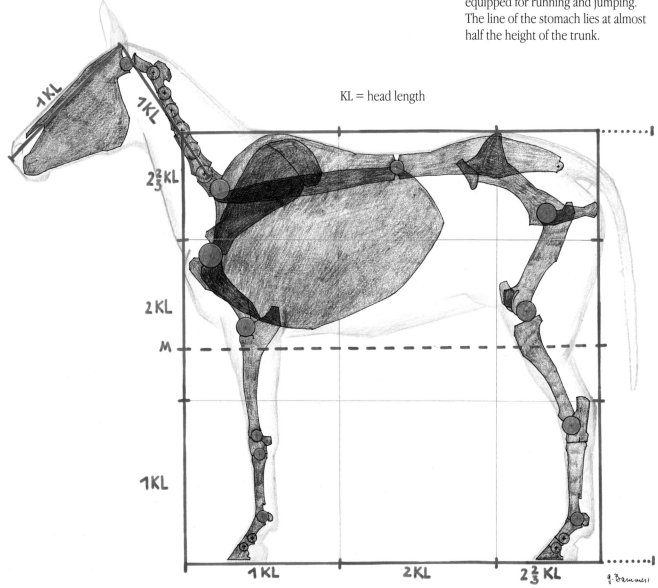

KL = head length

Another important distinguishing proportional feature, the dimensions of the thorax, must not be overlooked. All true quadrupeds that *walk on the ground* have a narrow, compressed thorax with great depth between the vertebral column and the sternum, which means that the forelegs can be suspended unimpeded along the sides of the thorax. Through evolution the ability of primates to stand in a semi-upright position has resulted in the thorax becoming square in cross-section, while upright human stance has caused a decrease in the depth of the thorax and an increase in its width (making it easier to maintain balance, see also fig. 11).

After this rough outline of proportion as a general distinguishing feature of animal form, we shall now see how proportion can be more exactly determined.

3.2
Establishing proportion – a practical quide

We first work out the regular proportional relationships of heights, lengths and widths, then compare them with one another and with the whole. This is called the *analogous* or *simultaneous* method.

The fact that the length of the trunk is greater than its height gives the animal's form a squat appearance, further reinforced by the fact that the elbow and knee are well above the outline of the stomach. NB: the head is carried at the same height as the rest of the back.

KL = head length

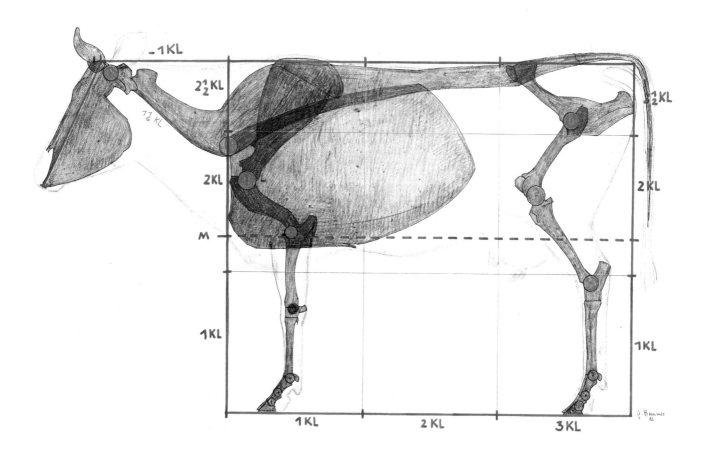

It is a good idea for beginners to use a basic module, such as the distance from the tip of the muzzle to behind the start of the ear (which also marks the rear limit of the skull). This distance, i.e. head length, is easy to measure on a living animal. The heights of the exposed part of each leg and the trunk and the length of the trunk can then be obtained in terms of this module. The withers (the elevation at the point where the back joins the neck) and croup (an elevation of the line of the back near the sacrum) are taken as the highest points of the trunk.

The length of the trunk is measured from the part of the chest that projects farthest at the front to the point on the hindquarters that projects farthest at the rear, i.e. the two ischial tuberosities (figs 23-26).

From these measurements it is possible to establish a characteristically proportioned rectangle based on the trunk, with essential factors and the height at which the trunk is carried. Other measurements such as neck length can also be obtained using the same module, or fractions of it.

● Use a profile view wherever possible.
● First establish the rectangle of the trunk, and only then add other information such as neck or head length or the height of the line of the stomach.

27 PROPORTIONAL
CHARACTERISTICS OF MAN
AND ANTHROPOID APE
(CHIMPANZEE)

Human proportions in the all-fours position highlight the shortness of the arms and great length of the legs. As a result the outline of the back drops as it approaches the head.

Primates that can climb, swing and hang have very long arms with which to grip and very short legs. As a result, the outline of the back slopes down towards the rear in a C shape.

KL = head length

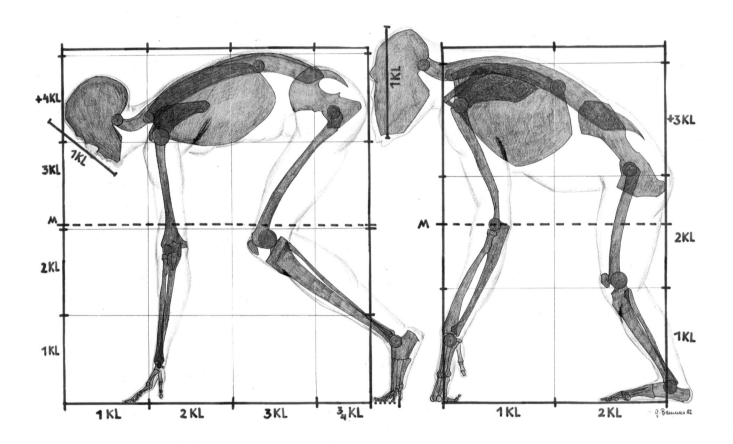

The sequence of steps for establishing proportion is as follows (fig. 29a-d):

- Use a compass or two pencils held like a compass to measure one head length from life (step 1, fig. 29**a**).
- Using the module you have just established, measure the height at the front of the trunk from the sole of the front hoof to the withers (step 2, fig. 29**a**). Result: height at withers, 2⅔H.
- Measure the length of the trunk in the same way (step 3, fig. 29**b**). Result: the length of the trunk of this horse is also 2⅔H.
- Establish the height at the rear of the trunk in the same way

(step 4, fig. 29c). Result: 2⅔H.

- Join all four points to form a rectangle (step 5, fig. 29d). Result: the rectangle so formed is here equivalent to a square.
- Draw a line half the height of the trunk (step 6, fig. 29d) and check whether the line of the stomach is above, below or at the same level as the halfway line.
- Determine neck length in terms of the head length module (step 7, fig. 29d), and draw in the head length as a directional line.

In this way we have established the rectangle formed by the trunk and legs, as well as the lengths of the neck and head. Fig. 29 offers ideas for further measurements.

28 COMPARISON OF THE PROPORTIONS OF A HUMAN BEING AND OF A GORILLA IN AN UNNATURALLY ERECT POSE

The makeup of the height and the width call for special attention. The human pelvis is considerably higher (longer legs). The gorilla's legs barely measure 2½H, while its arms are equivalent to 4 H.

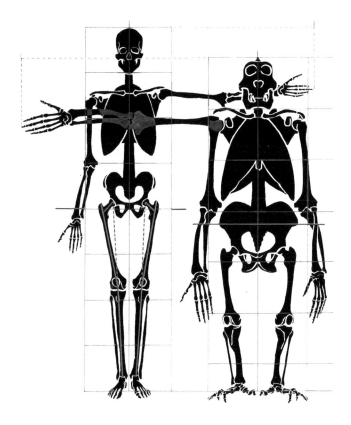

Immediately this proportional framework has been established work can start on the structure of the rest of the animal form, starting with the position of the limbs and the accents (e.g. the apexes of curves).

This procedure can be applied in just the same way to the forms of any and every mammal (figs 23-26), and can be simplified by estimating the trunk heights, then comparing them with one another and the estimated length of the trunk. In doing this you will gradually develop the ability to work freely, independently of exact measurements, an important preliminary step when working from life. You will learn to estimate, training the eye to assess measurements more and more reliably, resorting to exact measurement only occasionally when you are uncertain of something.

3.3
Practical work on proportion

We shall now assume that the preliminary exercises in measuring and establishing the rectangle formed by the trunk are behind us. When studies of proportion are carried out with a drawing material that can be applied rapidly and used on its side (e.g. red chalk), I would make the following recommendations (fig. 30):

- Choose a piece of red chalk that is the right length when applied on its side to convey the basic shape of the trunk in a single broad stroke (b, a). The length of the chalk will determine the eventual size of the study.
- The chalk should not be constantly lifted from the paper: convey the basic forms (including the limbs) in a single stroke.
- Experiment with swiveling the chalk round in an arc to produce triangular and trapezoid shapes (c), and use clear shapes such as these to build up whole limbs (d) and ultimately the entire animal form (e).

From this point on we can start including the first movements, still depicted two-dimensionally. If you doubt that it is possible to combine studies of proportion with movements, you may like to carry out the following small but very instructive diversion. Reinforce what you have learnt about proportion in figs 23-26 by making small, movable proportion blocks (fig. 31) of individual limbs with overlaps which can be used to make prints. Drill tiny holes in the blocks where the pivotal points are located – these must always match up when prints are made. If you put a small pin through these holes you can be sure that the next block will be placed in the right position directly overlapping the shape that has already been printed.

Please note:
- Any color can be used for printing. It is best to apply the paint or ink with a flat brush, then press down the shape as you would a block.
- Areas left blank in printing can add to the charm of the technique.
- The paint or ink need not be applied on the block evenly.
- It is always possible to overprint on an impression already made, perhaps using a different color.
- To make it clearer which legs are 'on top', i.e. nearer to the viewer, they should be printed more heavily.

Learning about proportion is a new, preparatory step toward expressing movement in repose and locomotive motion. Once we are also sure of the construction of the animal's framework, (see figs 4 and 8a-d), then we are well placed to tackle the next set of problems.

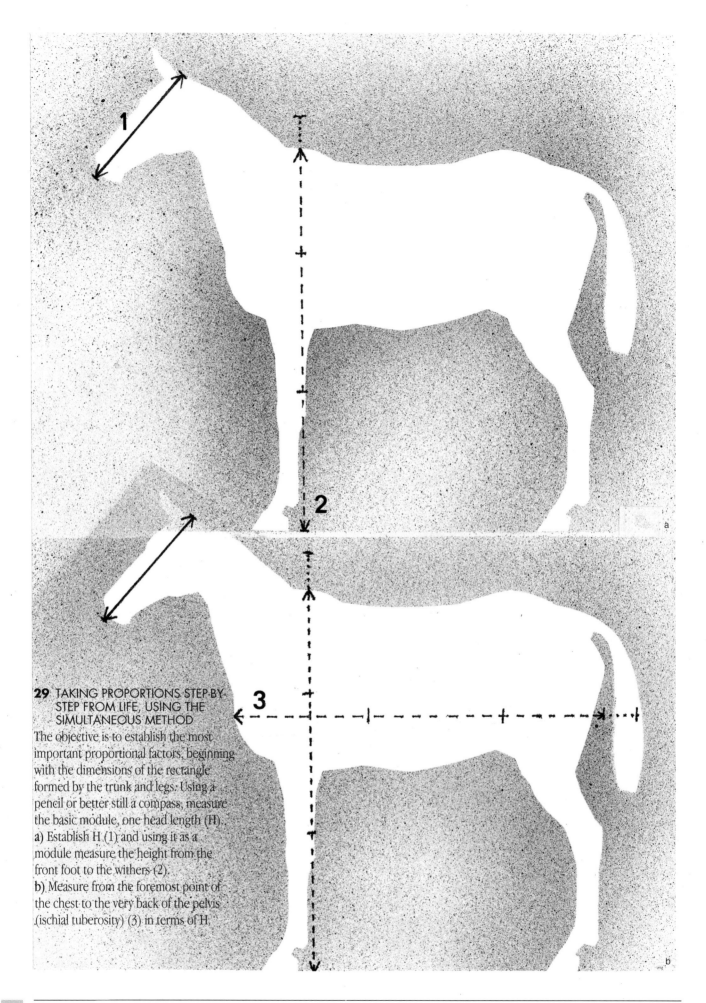

29 TAKING PROPORTIONS STEP-BY-STEP FROM LIFE, USING THE SIMULTANEOUS METHOD

The objective is to establish the most important proportional factors, beginning with the dimensions of the rectangle formed by the trunk and legs. Using a pencil or better still a compass, measure the basic module, one head length (H).

a) Establish H (1) and using it as a module measure the height from the front foot to the withers (2).

b) Measure from the foremost point of the chest to the very back of the pelvis (ischial tuberosity) (3) in terms of H.

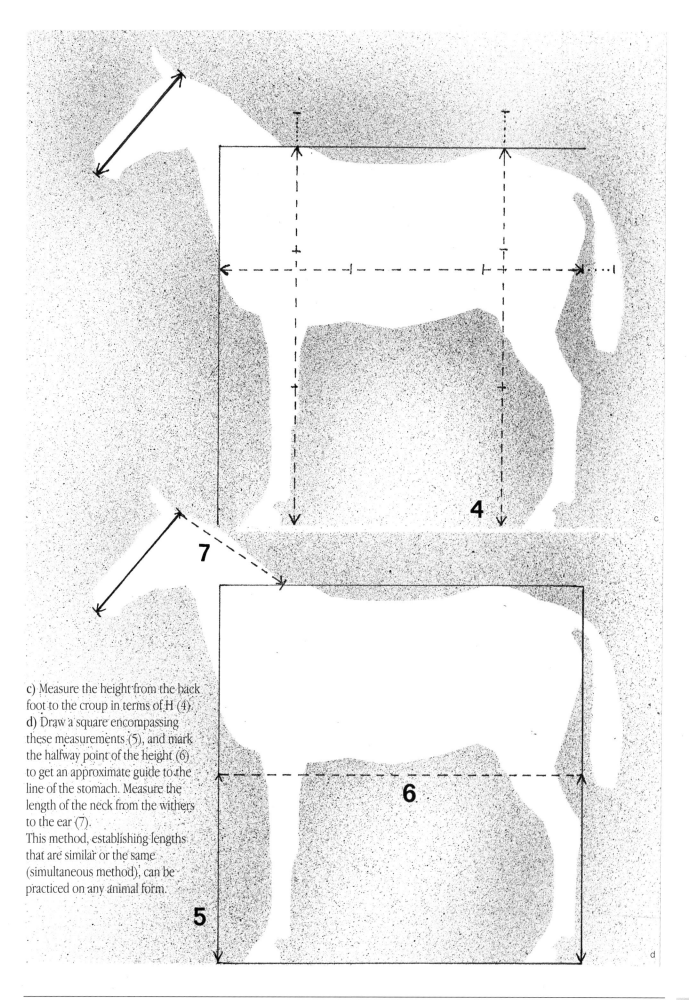

c) Measure the height from the back foot to the croup in terms of H (4).
d) Draw a square encompassing these measurements (5), and mark the halfway point of the height (6) to get an approximate guide to the line of the stomach. Measure the length of the neck from the withers to the ear (7).
This method, establishing lengths that are similar or the same (simultaneous method), can be practiced on any animal form.

30 TWO-DIMENSIONAL STUDIES
USING A BROAD MEDIUM

The purpose of the exercise is to use a
broad medium (red chalk) to convey
proportions quickly on paper in concise,
simple forms.

a, b) Conveying the mass of the trunk
with a piece of red chalk applied full
length on its side, and adding the rear
limbs in the same way.

c, d) The shapes making up the hind –
and forelegs produced by simply
swiveling the chalk.

e) The complete animal form – the way
in which the material was handled to give
virtually geometric shapes is still
discernible in the overlapping areas.

Red chalk on A3 paper

Section 3.2
Practical work on proportion

4.

Repose and motion – structural and dynamic rules

We are not entirely free to choose how to convey positions in repose involving movement or locomotive movements so that they are clearly understandable; how we make a standing position – whether on four legs or two – look like a standing position and not like a fall. What ultimately determines whether we perceive locomotive movement as hesitant, tripping or propped up is how the representation matches with natural laws. Repose and motion are both subject to the laws of gravity and always depend on the relationship between the center of gravity and the supporting surface. We must bear in mind that (fig. 32):

- A body's *center of gravity* is the notional center point of the body mass which is the only point that needs to be supported for the body to maintain its position in repose (balance).
- The *gravitational plumb line* (gravity line) runs straight down from the center of gravity, indicating the gravitational pull.
- The *supporting surface* (standing surface) is whatever the body is resting on in a standing, sitting or lying position.
- *Stability* is the resistance a body exerts on a horizontal supporting surface to being pushed or toppling over.
- *Balance* in repose obtains if the body's center of gravity is located over the supporting surface.

31 PRINTING IN COLOR WITH MOVABLE PROPORTIONED BLOCKS

Before preparing the blocks, the shapes and proportions of the chosen animal should have been established (fig. 25). When applying paint or ink to the blocks with a brush you can graduate the intensity and shade, or partially overprint an impression already made in a different color.

Print using acrylic paints on A4-size paper

Compared with human stability, animal stability is extremely good because:

- the standing surface covered by an animal's four feet is large;
- its center of gravity is low;
- its stability increases as the body weight rises.

If for any reason the center of gravity goes outside the supporting surface the body loses its balance and falls over in the direction in which the center of gravity is displaced (the tipping edge). An animal's center of gravity is in the front third of the body (fig. 32), and if the body is shifted backward or forward it can move over the supporting surface, with the various axes of the body (the alignment of the pelvis, the trochanter major on either side and the points of the shoulder blades) still remaining horizontal (fig. 33). But the axis shift into slanting positions if the body ceases to be supported evenly on all four feet.

4.1
Modes of standing, sitting and lying

What happens functionally in the standing position changes when the standing surface is reduced (to standing on three or two feet, figs 34, 35). The whole organism makes an immediate and continuous endeavor to equalize forces. It reacts sensitively to slight changes in the relationship between the position of the center of gravity and the size of the supporting surface. These changes can arise from the need to off-load weight and relax (fig. 35) when one leg is lifted or the neck is bent sideways. What are the essential *changes in form* that result from counterbalancing weight?

- When the body is supported on three feet in walking (lifting of the front swinging leg, fig. 34) the center of gravity must be shifted sideways so as to be above the supporting leg.
- Consequently the supporting leg is in a slanting position.
- The point of the shoulder blade on the side of the supporting leg is higher than that on the unsupported side.
- When the body is supported on three feet in a standing position with one of the hindlegs carrying no weight (a typical relaxing attitude in the horse), the weight-bearing hindleg is in a more slanting position, and the pelvis drops toward the unsupported side (fig. 35b). This is comparable to what happens to a human being in a contrapposto position (fig. 35a).
- The decreased distance between the pelvis and the ground is reflected by the trailing leg inevitably taking up a compensatory position: i.e. there is greater flexing at the joints.

We find particularly striking changes in form in the standing position of a cat washing its raised front paw. The shoulder blade on the weight-bearing opposite side protrudes sharply. When a horse is standing on its hindlegs (the levade position) the muscles in the hindquarters have to exert a powerful effort to pull the body's center of gravity sharply back above the rear hoofs. Stable balance is turned into labile balance.

There are two main modes of sitting: *sitting upright* on the hindquarters end without any support from the forelegs (apes, bears) and *sitting on the haunches* (fig. 36a, linear outline) with the supporting forelegs straightened for structural reasons. The main features of changing from a standing position to sitting on the haunches are (fig. 36):

- The forelegs stay more or less where they are (fig. 36a).
- The hindlegs bend at the joints, the top sections of the legs (the femur and tibia) touch one another, and are brought up near the supporting forelegs.
- The vertebral column as it extends from the thoracic to the lumbar vertebrae forms a C-shape with a clear hump.

The transition from *sitting on the haunches to a lying position* differs from one species to another (dogs and cats, fig. 36a):

- The hindlegs stay where they are, but are brought closer together.
- The front part of the body is pushed forward. The forelegs lie straight out from the paw to the elbow. The sternum helps support the weight.

The transition from a *standing to a lying position* (fig. 36b) goes as follows:

- The front and back paws remain where they are.
- All joints fold up simultaneously, but the front part of the body slides back a little.
- The vertebral column bends between the thoracic and lumbar sections.

An intermediate mode between standing and lying (in cats) is the *mousing position* where the body is half crouching and half squatting (e.g. when feeding), with the feet tucked under the body. From this crouching position the joints can suddenly jerk into a standing and springing position. When hoofed animals are in a lying position (fig. 37) the fetlock joint bends sharply so that the front feet can tuck up under the cannon bone. The back foot is rolled to one side of the rear shank.

32 POSITION OF THE CENTER OF GRAVITY AND HOW IT SHIFTS

The low-lying center of gravity (red dot) above a supporting surface that is constant in size gives the animal good equilibrium and great stability. If the body is moved forward or backward the center of gravity can shift considerably (see pale gray outlines). The continuous red line is the gravity line, which falls within the standing surface.

33 POSITION OF THE CENTER OF GRAVITY AND ITS IMPACT ON PLASTIC ACCENTS (MARKED IN RED)

When the animal's weight is supported evenly on all four feet the axes of important corresponding plastic accents are horizontal.

a) Rear view, marking the position of the croup, the hip tuberosities, and great trochanters.

b) Front view, marking the regular horizontal alignment of the points of the shoulder blades.

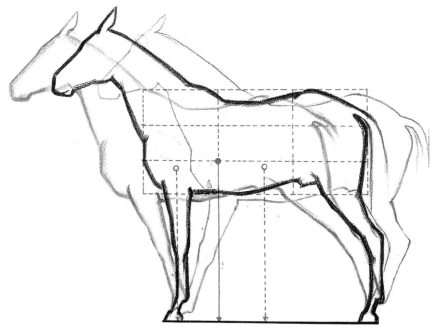

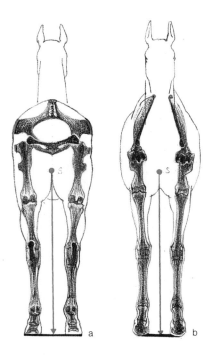

Section 4.1
Modes of standing, sitting and lying

4.2
Modes of locomotive movement

The body in repose often makes *behavioral movements* which do not involve moving from place to place.

Locomotive movement, from one place to another, is effected by thrust from the hindlegs. The center of gravity located forward the front is pushed forward beyond the standing surface, and a fall is prevented by one of the forelegs moving ahead. Thus the thrust always comes from behind. How does the thrust occur?

- The hindleg that is farthest forward (fig. 38) becomes the one that propels movement as the joints extend. The propelling or bracing leg transmits power via the hip joint onto the pelvis.
- Meanwhile the other hindleg (the swinging leg) is lifted off the ground and in a slightly flexed position swings like a pendulum past the support point of the leg providing the thrust and extends as it prepares to touch the ground (becoming in turn the bracing leg).

The procedure described is fundamental, and applies to both *four-time movement* and the *amble*. Either of these main gaits of the horse can change in tempo from a stride to a trot, gallop or jump.

The characteristics of the stride in *four-time movement* are the alternating combinations of the legs that provide bipedal support (fig. 38):

- At the outset the animal is supported on three legs (phase 1) with one leg raised at the front; this is followed by *diagonal support* provided by one weight-bearing foreleg and one weight-bearing hindleg on opposite sides of the body (phase 2). The diagonally opposite swinging legs are moving forward.
- The forward-moving swinging foreleg touches the ground so that there is now a supporting leg at both back and front on the same side of the body (phase 3).

34 STRUCTURAL AND FUNCTIONAL EFFECTS WHEN A FORELEG IS RAISED

The reduction of the standing surface to just one leg at the front and two at the back necessitates a sideways shift of the center of gravity towards the supporting foot, pushing the whole supporting leg into a very slanting position. As a result there are twists in the longitudinal axes of the trunk seen in section.

35 STRUCTURAL AND FUNCTIONAL EFFECTS WHEN ONE HINDLEG CARRIES NO WEIGHT

These effects are similar to those described in fig. 34, and are similar to the human pose with one standing leg and one trailing leg (**a**). Because of a lack of support the standing leg must again adopt a slanting position as the center of gravity shifts, and the pelvis on the unsupported side drops down (**b**). The trailing leg is therefore forced to take up a compensating position (the joints are bent, and the foot may be placed in front).

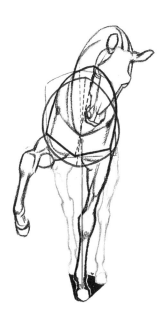

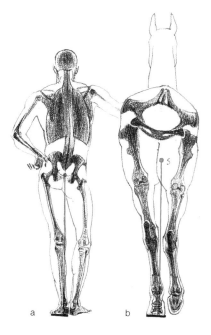

36 TWO MODES OF LYING DOWN

a) In moving from a sitting to a lying position the front of the body is pushed forward and the forelegs laid flat from the elbows to the pads of the feet, while the hindlegs are tightly folded.

b) In moving from a standing to a lying position, the forefeet stay in position while the rear of the body is pushed back, and the hindlegs then fold down.

37 STUDIES OF POSITIONS IN REPOSE (NILGAI ANTELOPE)

The animal's slender limbs and rapidly changing positions are best depicted with a material that can be used flat but is also capable of outlining delicate shapes with a single line.

Red chalk on A3-size gray paper

Section 4.2
Modes of locomotive movement

Movement continues as follows:

● Changeover to the reverse diagonal bipedally supported position (phase 4). The front of the foot nearest to view now lies a long way back, and the opposite hindleg is a long way forward, while the leg that is about to give the next forward thrust is still swinging.

Thus in the *walking gait* in four-time movement there are *six main phases*:

● *Phase 1*: Starting off supported on three feet, with two points of support at the back.
● *Phase 2*: Diagonal bipedal support from a foreleg and a hindleg on opposite sides of the body.
● *Phase 3*: Bipedal support from a fore- and hindleg on the same side of the body.
● *Phase 4*: Change to diagonal bipedal support from opposite sides of the body, reversing the leg position in phase 2.
● *Phase 5*: Support on three feet, with two points of support at the front and one at the back.

● *Phase 6*: Bipedal support from a fore- and hindleg on the same side of the body (the opposite side from that supported in phase 3).

When the limbs on one side of the body are lifted at the same time while the opposite side takes on the supporting function, this is described as an *ambling gait* (elephant, bear, grayhound, giraffe, camel). Big cats do not as a rule alternate support as in the four-time movement just described but when excited both they and dogs sometimes change to an ambling gait. The cow though basically an animal that uses four-time movement is always half-ambling.

The *trot* is next in speed to the walking gait (fig. 39), and follows the same principles in the sequence of support. However, the greater thrust exerted by the hindlegs throws the body forward so powerfully that between the points where it is supported diagonally on one side and then on the other there is a phase where no leg is touching the ground (*suspension phase*).

38 PHASES IN THE STRIDE IN FOUR-TIME MOVEMENT SHOWING THE GRAVITY LINE
These diagrams of the horse's walking gait indicate where the feet touch the ground (solid black), together with the standing surface applicable in each case. The positions of the swinging legs are outlined in black.

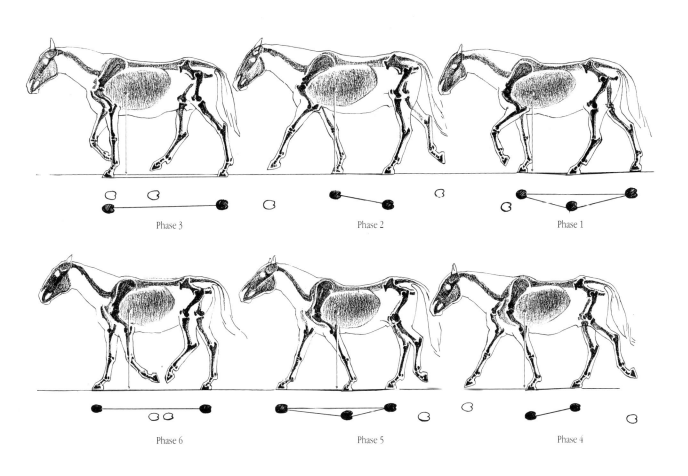

Phase 3   Phase 2   Phase 1

Phase 6   Phase 5   Phase 4

Main phases of the trot (fig. 39)
- *Phase 1*: The body is thrown forward and supported diagonally, BL (back left) – FR (front right).
- *Phase 2*: The two supporting legs, BL-FR, are lifted, transition to the suspension phase.
- *Phase 3*: The two diagonally opposite legs which were swinging in phase 1 are set down to give diagonal bipedal support.
- *Phase 4*: Transition to the suspension phase.
- *Phase 5*: As Phase 3, on opposite feet.
- *Phase 6*: Same feet on the ground as in Phase 5; near fore and off hind swing forward.

In the trot three legs never touch the ground simultaneously.

The *gallop* (fig. 40): This is the fastest form of locomotive movement, and involves a leaping action. The movement of the legs on the right and left of a central line is not identical. The lively forward thrust on the frontquarters means that one or both forelegs are required to support the oscillation (transmitting the body's centrifugal force). The body is launched still further forward past the supporting leg so that it too has to

be lifted off the ground (suspension phase). At that point first one hindleg, then the other, makes contact with the ground.
Main phases of the gallop
- *Phase 1*: The body is supported on three feet, BL, BR and FR.
- *Phase 2*: BR becomes a swinging leg: diagonal bipedal support, BL and FR. FL gets ready to touch the ground.
- *Phase 3*: Support on one foot.
- *Phase 4*: Lifting of this bracing leg leads to the suspension phase.
- *Phase 5*: Forward movement of the hindlegs which touch the ground shortly after one another.
- *Phase 6*: FR also touches the ground so that the body is again supported on three feet.

For thousands of years before the invention of photography there was confusion among artists as to the actions actually involved in locomotive movement. The problem of depicting the gallop was wrongly resolved by showing the two hindlegs braced as if the horse were about to jump, with the two forelegs both raised off the ground and bent at the fetlock, or stretched forward as if the horse were making a high, wide jump.

39 PHASES OF THE TROT
The sequence reads from right to left. In contrast to the walking pace which is never in suspension, in the trot a suspension phase succeeds the diagonally supported start. It is in turn followed by reverse diagonal bipedal contact with the ground, etc.

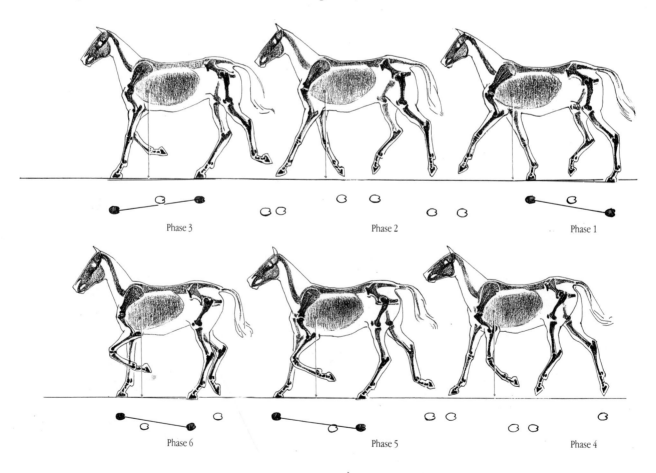

Phase 3   Phase 2   Phase 1

Phase 6   Phase 5   Phase 4

Section 4.2
Modes of locomotive movement

The dog moving full tilt (fig. 41)
The front of the body is brought close to the hindlegs that provide the thrust, then the body is gradually catapulted forward with the forelegs at first flexed. With the powerful extension of all their joints the hindlegs too leave the ground (suspension phase). The forelegs are brought down by a powerful flexing of the elbow joint and reach down to touch the ground. Meanwhile the two hindlegs 'overtake' the forelegs, touching down well ahead of them. The vertebral column which is hunched up contributes to the moving process by flexing, then shooting out like a tension spring as it extends, so supporting a long forward reach by the forelegs.

The horse's jump (fig. 42)
The jump can be executed from the trot or the gallop. The hindlegs are flexed to give thrust. The whole body including the neck area is raised up, and the front limbs are tightly flexed. The upward and forward impetus leads to the suspension phase. The tight flexing of the forelegs is relaxed. Finally the two forelegs are extended to receive the impact of landing. The hindlegs are now flexed and tucked into the body, while the vertebral column forms a concave curve near the loins and the neck is retracted.

This demonstrates the need to position the front parts of the body well forward at lift-off, adopt an intermediate position for all parts of the body in the suspension phase, and retract the neck sharply on landing (balance).

The cat leaping from a crouching position (fig. 43)
- The body is lowered, the vertebral column hunched and the hind legs bent up beneath the middle of the body.
- Push-off from behind, with the fore-limbs still drawn into the body.
- Extension of the hindlegs and the vertebral column.
- The suspension phase as the hindlegs are further extended and the forelegs are brought forward.
- The body's centrifugal force is absorbed on landing by marked flexing of the shoulder- and elbow-joints. The joints of the hindlegs are bent to draw them forward under the body.

40 PHASES OF THE GALLOP
The sequence reads from right to left. The leaping locomotive movement starts with three hoofs touching the ground, then two diagonal feet, next a single support, then a suspension phase, followed by first one hindleg and then the other being brought forward and set down. Finally the foreleg touches the ground again as at the outset.

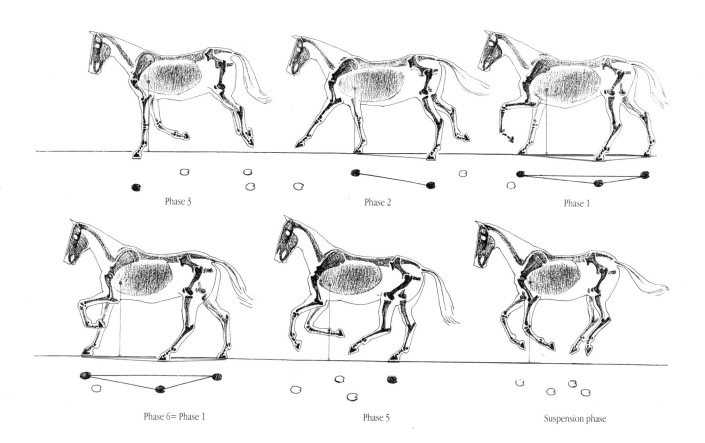

Phase 3   Phase 2   Phase 1

Phase 6= Phase 1   Phase 5   Suspension phase

41 PHASES OF THE MOVEMENT OF A DOG MOVING FULL TILT

The sequence reads from right to left. The most important features: both hindlegs push off, the whole body shoots out during the suspension phase, the two forelegs touch the ground and the hindlegs come forward to touch down ahead of them, with the back forming a pronounced curve.

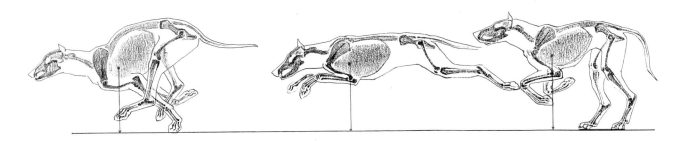

42 THE HORSE'S JUMP SHOWN IN THREE PHASES

The sequence reads from right to left. The most important features: both hindlegs push off while the forelegs are tightly flexed; the suspension phase with the legs less tightly flexed to almost the same extent at front and back; landing on the extended forelegs, with the hindlegs tightly flexed.

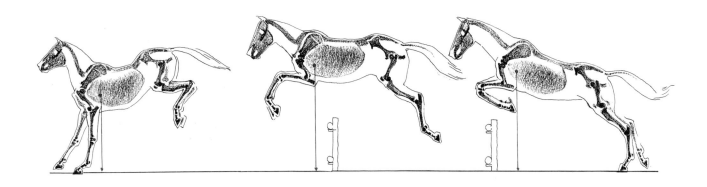

43 PHASES IN THE SPRING OF A CAT

The sequence reads from right to left. From a crouching position: the hindlegs push off while the forelegs are drawn up to the trunk; the body shoots out; in the suspension phase the whole body is fully extended; the cat lands on its forelegs while the hindlegs are drawn up to the trunk.

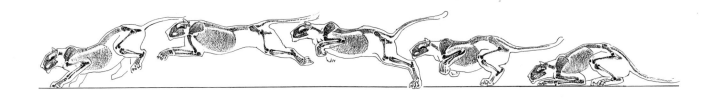

44 PHASES IN THE AMBLING GAIT
OF THE GIRAFFE
The sequence reads from right to left,
demonstrating how the legs are lifted
each time on the same side, which results
in a slightly swaying gait.

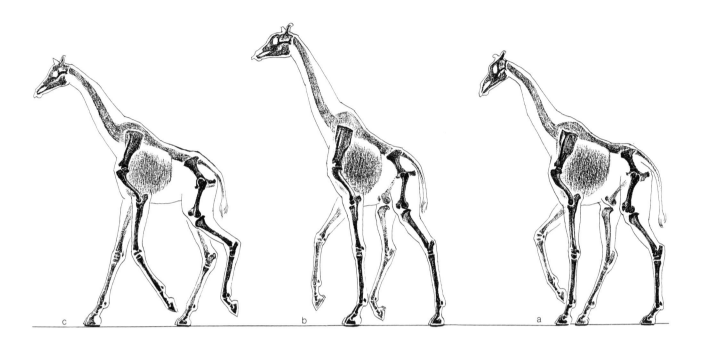

4.3
Exercises in repose and motion

When looking at practical work on proportion we were able to show that our approach opened the door to the integration of proportion and locomotive movement. We now return to this idea, but first some more advice for positions in repose.

Once again an informed choice of medium can make it easier to draw systematically. Knowledge, experience and skills already acquired are practiced and reinforced in combined work on proportion and positions in repose and motion. It is best to select difficulties down to a minimum. *Here again we ask what the different materials can do for us, what language they speak:*

- Broad, dry materials (chalks) facilitate not only rapid work, but the concentration of larger masses (fig. 45).

- Similarly, the movable proportioned block could again be used. If the combination of proportion and movement is considered overtaxing the expression of movement alone could be concentrated on first.

- A watercolor brush (figs 46-50) can catch positions in repose with movement fluently and smoothly in a matter of seconds.

- Pointed drawing implements such as a pen, pencil or felt-tip

encourage a free approach when drawing from life or working from imagination (fig. 51).

The wet medium of watercolor, quick and responsive, can excellently convey the fleeting expression of movement. You have to be a little patient with yourself, for you will not achieve the results you want without taking time to train and accumulate experience. The round watercolor brush has to obey at just the right moment like one of the fingers of the hand. Drawing with a watercolor brush (figs 46-50) involves:

- The ability to work quickly.
- Concentration on the expression of movement.
- The continuity and flow of an uninterrupted method of working.
- A high degree of concentrated observation.
- The training of visual memory.
- Sympathetic insight into the essence of movement.
- Pressure to use shorthand abbreviations and avoid getting bogged down in detail.

When drawing with a watercolor brush avoid:
- Breaking off and improving. It is better to start again.
- A mismatch between too big a picture and too small a brush.
- Drawing a preliminary outline with the brush and filling it in.

Materials needed when drawing with a watercolor brush:
- Use a brush that absorbs a generous amount of water, is flexible, responds quickly to pressure and still has a good point.
- Have plenty of transparent watercolor paint ready mixed.
- Choose a color that suits the color of your paper.

Again do not attempt to make a silhouette outline!

a

45 A COMPLEX AND DIFFERENTIATED DEPICTION IN REPOSE WITH CHALK

a) Disregarding details, the outline is primarily established as a triangular shape, applying the chalk in broad strokes. The angular shapes result from deliberately keeping the edges of the chalk strokes sharp and unblurred.
Medium-hard black chalk on A4-size kraft paper

A successful working method with watercolor (figs 46-50):

- Preliminary drawings would cancel out the meaning of the work.
- The shape of the animal should be drawn from head to hindleg without a break.
- Where forms overlap or intersect, separating lines should be omitted.
- The different forms and their intensity should emerge from varying the pressure with which the brush is applied.
- Pressing, trailing, turning and pulling all contribute toward a personal style for each artist.
- Application and practice are indispensable, particularly at this point.
- The profile view is preferable to practice brush technique, providing the best opportunity of drawing freely (fig. 46). If three-dimensional views cannot be avoided (fig. 47) it is best to use blank areas to suggest formal articulation.

b) The principles used in drawing (**a**) are retained in this two-color study. Mass and solidity are built up, and contrasts reinforced. More attention is paid to individual shapes.
Bistre and red chalk on A3-size kraft paper

b

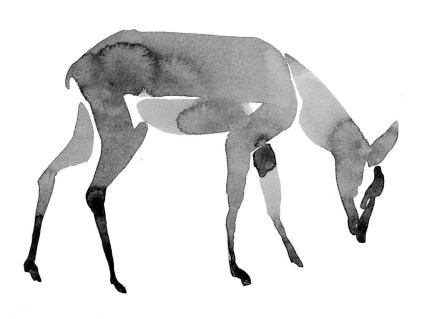

46 STUDY OF MOVEMENT USING A BRUSH

Whether an animal model is present or not, the study should be executed in a single, consecutive stroke in a matter of seconds. Straightforward profile views are recommended to start with.

Round watercolor brush and watercolor paint on A4-size paper

47 BRUSH STUDIES WITH FORESHORTENING

Foreshortening, covered areas and intersections in three-dimensional views or where several animals partly conceal one another are difficult to convey using a single application of the brush as the constituent forms have to be separated by blank areas; otherwise the result can be an amorphous mass.

Watercolor brush and watercolor paint on A4-size watercolor paper

48-50 BRUSH STUDIES OF THREE-DIMENSIONAL VIEWS

The comments on fig. 47 apply here too. Brush studies executed really smoothly with no 'spluttering' are a superb means of capturing the essence of movement. Work from a Bammes teacher's further training course, Schule für Gestaltung, Zurich.

Watercolor brush and watercolor paint on A3-size paper

51 TRAINING THE VISUAL IMAGINATION

No exploration of a problem area should be regarded as completed until knowledge and ability have been tested in graphic work from imagination. This tests the certainty with which we can conjure up what we know, more readily reveals what has not been understood, and encourages creative experiment.

Drawing pen and Indian ink on A4-size paper

52 VISUAL MEMORY AND VISUALIZING

Capturing the expression of movement that takes place in a matter of seconds involves visual memory, visual experience and imaginative power. It is possible to improve all these, especially if the artist is sure of the processes of movement.
Franz Marc (1880-1916), Leaping horse from behind, and Two views of a leaping horse in profile, 1910.

Pen and Indian ink, 4 x 12¼ in (10 x 30.8 cm)

Section 4.3
Exercises in repose and motion

4.4

Freedom – improvisation – experiment

The student should now be aware of increasing freedom and a looser approach, the freedom to omit, should have the ability to take in all that is happening in a movement at a single glance and work spontaneously. The boundaries become fluid. Though it is important not to let everything learned so far slip away, the aim now is to work unpretentiously and without a fixed purpose: this is free play, therapy, an entertaining pastime, so you travel light. Rather than setting out to draw phase 3 of a horse in a field, you should simply start drawing and make something of whatever comes. You can use whatever you have to hand: write in the sand, scribble in the margin of a newspaper or on a paper napkin. Forget all the highfalutin stuff!

The following suggestions are made for spontaneous work (fig. 51):

- Use whatever implements you are most familiar with.
- As you want to draw what you feel immediately, the size of the animal form should be kept suitably small, clear and compact (saving time).
- Large outlines call for lavish elaboration, otherwise they often do not work two-dimensionally because they appear empty.
- An instrument that produces fine lines has a fixed relationship

with the size of the figure, but it can also be useful for conveying delicacy.

- A lavish, elaborate result is not expected from spontaneous work in which the imagination and a sense of the essential are nurtured.
- Be bold in your search for form. Do not worry about drawing in a line a second or third time.
- Openness of presentation is also part of improvisation: ultimate solutions and final definitions have no place here.

Conveying a sense of movement – easily recognizable in the work of such masters as Franz Marc (fig. 52) or Josef Hegenbarth (fig. 53) – requires another expressive component which might be called 'sharpness of movement'. Incomplete work, not comprehensive and fully detailed, in fact conveys to the observer a sense of rapid movement which cannot be perceived in total clarity. Even modern photography has given up trying to freeze a view of cascading droplets of water into a thousandth of a second. In sketches of ideas by the great masters of graphic art it is often in fact the improvised, freshly recorded movement that is truthful and convincing in its *non finito*, its lacunae, its openness to possibilities and its intimations. As Toulouse-Lautrec, Delacroix, Steinlen or Hegenbarth so tellingly demonstrate, the use of medium too should follow the actual or imagined experience of movement with free, light nimbleness.

However, it would be a mistake to think that everything jotted down with such seeming effortlessness had no source other than pure spontaneity, sudden impulse and an ardent temperament. *All great proficiency is based on an immense store of visual experience and knowledge of how things fit together.* Investigation of proportion and the problems of forms assumed in repose and motion are very much resolved by a complex view, to a large extent ignoring detail. However, without the enrichment and enhancement that a thorough acquaintance with individual forms provides, the repertory of forms is soon exhausted. The practical knowledge offered in the following chapters thus serves to provide that essential increased store of information, so that new skills can be fed into the stream of graphic expertise.

53 MOVEMENT RECORDED IN SHORTHAND

Sketching is always a test of whether an essential has been understood – here movement seems almost to have been perceived by a somnambulist. This expressiveness was the artist's only concern in leaving out all non-essentials. Thus a quick scribble becomes a solution that is complete in itself.

Josef Hegenbarth (1884-1962), Horse rearing.

Pencil study in the possession of the artist's widow

Section 4.4
Freedom – improvisation – experiment

5.

The forms of the hindleg

Familiarity with the most important aspects of anatomical structure is a major object of our study, starting with a review of the structural and dynamic components of the skeleton and concluding with the arrangement of the various groups of muscles. Both are keys to a practical understanding of form for graphic purposes, using observation, knowledge and skill to weld visual experiences together into an indivisible whole.

5.1
Drawing the construction of the skeleton

It is helpful at this point to bear in mind what has already been said about overall construction (chapter 1, section 3) and the forces that release movement (chapter 4, section 2). The hindleg is adapted to its structural and dynamic function in a number of basic formal characteristics relating to fitness for purpose (fig. 54), including:
- the nature of its articulation;
- its greater length in absolute terms compared with the foreleg (except in brachiating animals);
- the number, make-up and sequence of the angular joints;
- the special structure with joints located so as to save muscle power;
- the specific dimensions of the musculature in relation to particular joints;
- the way in which the foot is specialized and developed.

All these factors, which are directly or indirectly accessible to the eye, have an influence on the structure of form.

The two hindlegs form the rear support of the bridge construction (see chapter 1, fig.5), and combine with the pelvis to become the body's *center of movement*. They also play an important role in species-specific proportions (the shape of the rectangle formed by the trunk – see chapter 3, figs 23-27).

Evolutionary changes in way of life have led to changes in the position and relationship of the limbs to the ground:
- Plantigrades evolved into digitigrades, e.g. animals of prey walking on the end sections of the metatarsus (fig. 23), and unguligrades (hoofed animals) that walk on the end joints of the digits (hoof).
- The stilt-like upright position of the foot of the unguligrade was accompanied by considerable elongation of the metatarsus (figs 54a, b).

The number and sequences of joint angles are the same in the hindlegs of all mammals, in line with the push-off function they perform (fig. 54a), but the angles vary. When the legs are extended (pushed off from the ground) the angles increase, and when they are flexed the angles decrease. The angles in question are:
- the angle at the hip joint between the pelvis and the femur; open to the front;
- the angle at the femuro-tibial joint; open to the back;
- the angle of the tarsal joint between the tibia and the metatarsus; open to the front;
- the angle of the first digital joint; open to the front.

The angles of the joints, which are very striking in profile, contribute to expressing the dynamic nature of their form, in conjunction with the groups of muscles associated with them (fig. 59). These two factors combine to produce the curving shape of the limbs. The decisive axes of movement (pivotal points) are the dominant features: in animals that run well these are the cross-axes (at right angles to the direction of movement) which are characteristic of hinge joints and make flexion and extension possible (fig. 56). While flexing and extending are in progress the formal appearance of the joints and the direction of the sides of the angles alter, especially from the femuro-tibial joint downward:
- The angle of the extended femuro-tibial joint in association with the contour of the muscles is obtuse (fig. 56a),
- and when flexed it is broken into several facets because in the femuro-tibial joint the fossa and condyles of the femur roll over the tibia in a backward movement.

In terms of drawing this means that the shape of the femuro-tibial joint appears particularly massive and obtuse (fig. 56b).
- The angle of the extended tarsal joint is very shallow, so that the calcaneum can be seen protruding vertically.
- When the tarsal joint is flexed it closes to form an acute angle, and the calcaneum sticks out noticeably toward the back (fig. 56b).
- The first, second and third phalanges of the digits are far more capable of being flexed than of being extended.

All this implies that the possibilities of movement as we come to the end sections of the leg are increasingly confined to fine-tuning the way the foot is used, though the broad outlines of its movement are decided high up at the hip joint; in animals that run well the hip joint's essential mechanics are restricted to bending and stretching (flexion and extension).

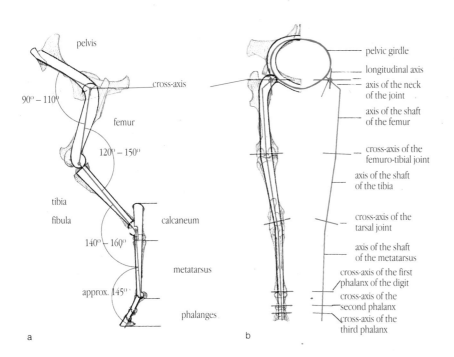

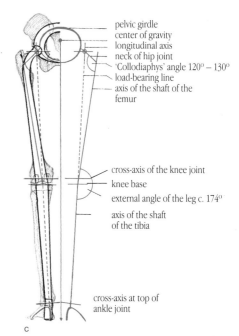

a

b

c

54 SIMILARITIES AND DIFFERENCES IN THE ARTICULATION OF AN ANIMAL'S HINDLEG (A, B) AND THE HUMAN LEG (C)

The number of sections in both forms of leg is the same, and there is little difference in their constructional lines in front or back view. In profile however there are considerable differences, notably the marked angularity of the animal leg as an extensible device providing forward thrust.

The outline drawing shows how the main articulated forms connect, and the gray shading shows the subsidiary forms articulating from the constructional connections.

55 PELVIS OF A HERBIVORE (HORSE) INDICATING POINTS THAT HAVE AN IMPACT ON SURFACE MODELING

Between the areas marked in red there are layers of hip and rump muscle that fill the space staked out by the skeletal shape. Three-quarter rear view, seen externally from the left.

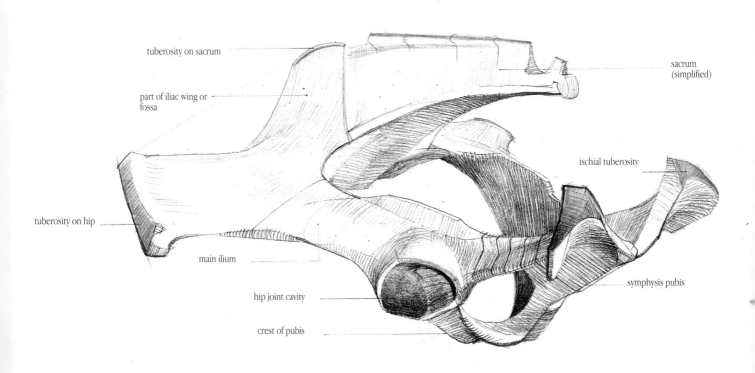

Section 5.1
Drawing the construction of the skeleton

56 THE PLASTIC EFFECTS OF THE MECHANICS OF THE KNEE

It is important for the graphic artist to have some knowledge of the mechanical changes that take place in the femuro-tibial joint to get a clear understanding of the various forms it can assume:

a) The femuro-tibial joint in a relatively extended resting position forms an accent at the meeting point of an obtuse angle (the accent results from the position of the patell**a**).

b) The flexed joint as it turns and rolls produces a virtual right angle the sides of which meet at the patella.

c) When the joint is extremely flexed and the condyles of the femur are turned round their own axis without locomotive movement, the angle between the femur and the tibia is sharply produced.

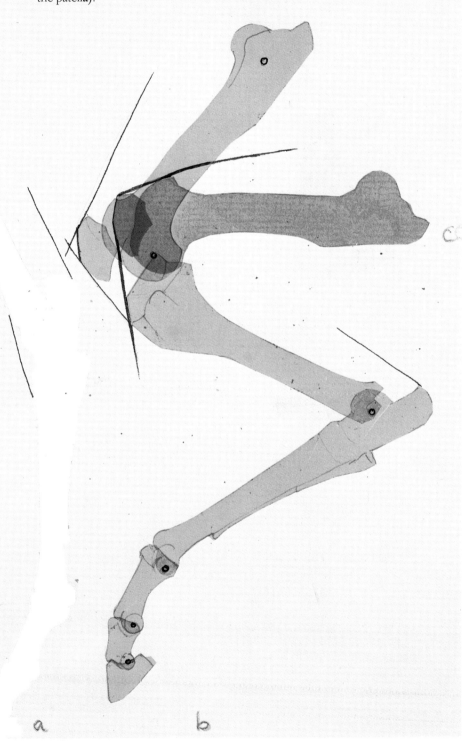

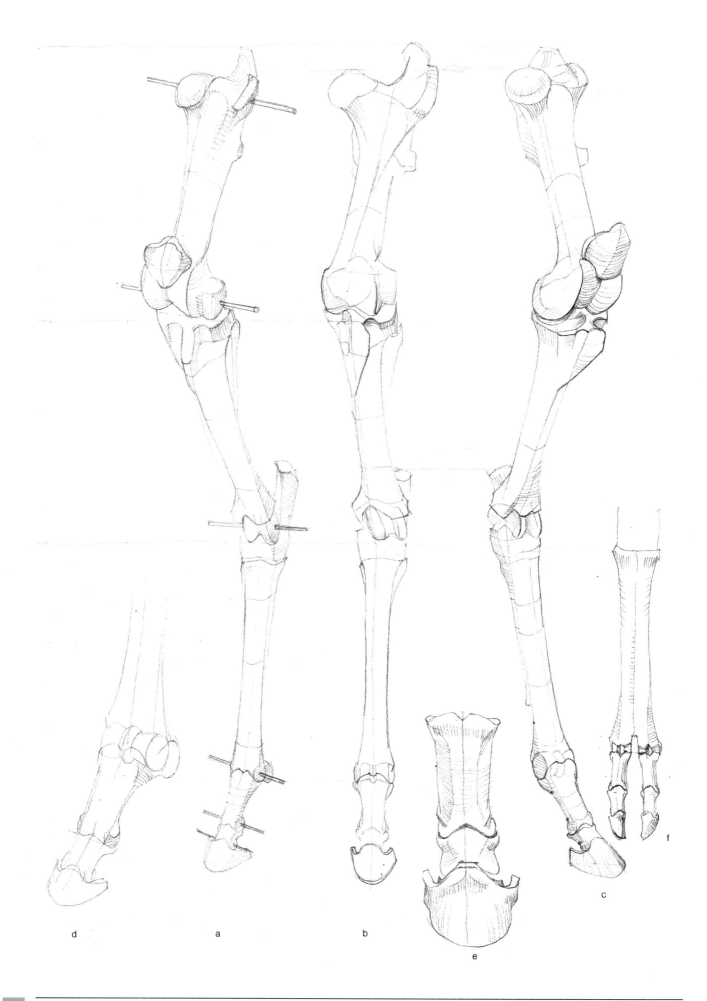

d   a   b   c   e   f

Section 5.1
Drawing the construction of the skeleton

57 DRAWING THE SKELETAL
STRUCTURE OF A HORSE'S
HINDLEG

a) Basic directions of the sections of the
leg and their pivotal points.
b) The subsidiary forms and the joint axes
are added to the skeletal outline;
dimensions decrease in size the further
down the leg we travel.
c-f) The forms of the foot and the digits
merit particularly careful study.

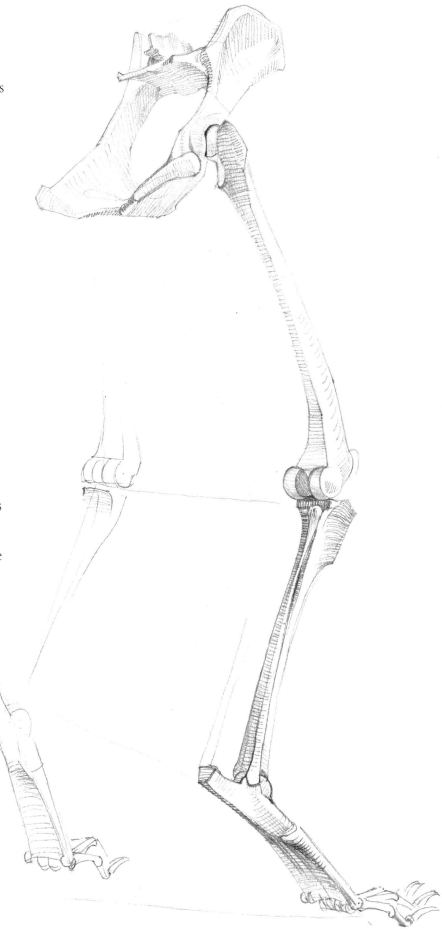

58 DRAWING THE SKELETAL
STRUCTURE OF THE HINDLEG OF
A MEMBER OF THE DOG FAMILY
(WOLF)

Virtually the same procedure is followed
as in fig. 57. The three-dimensional,
three-quarter rear view of the foot affords
a view of the shallow vaulting of the
metatarsus (depicted as a complex
entity), which is hollow on the side of the
sole.

Model study drawn by the author at a
Bammes teachers' further training
course, Schule für Gestaltung, Zurich,
A4 paper

The formal characteristics relating to movement and mechanics are much less striking in the front and rear views (figs 54b, c). We are instead aware of *structure*, a qualitatively different characteristic of form. The leg's supporting nature emerges because the pronounced angles associated with the profile view are absent. The form taken by the skeleton of an animal's leg (fig. 54b) is not totally dissimilar to the human leg (fig. 54c).

As the center of movement and sculptural core of the rear of the trunk the pelvis requires careful observation (fig. 55):

● Branching off from the closed circular construction are the sculptural shapes of the hip bone with the hip tuberosity sticking out at the side toward the front, and the tuberosity of the sacrum (the croup) at the top,

● the ischial tuberosities at the rear,

● and at the front above, the protective spine of the sacrum.

The stable annular construction of the pelvis slopes forward at a shallow angle, receiving the arch of the vertebral column and virtually continuing it, and transmits the thrust of the leg onto the vertebral column by way of the top of the hip joint embedded into the hip-joint cavity.

Unless you are completely sure of the structure of the leg, you should make a graphic study of the essential forms of an actual skeleton, following a set sequence of working steps.

The skeleton of the hindleg of an ungulate (horse) is used to illustrate certain points (fig. 57):

● the simplified form of joint condyles and/or ball joints (**a**);

● their positions relative to one other and the associated joint angles;

● the progressive narrowing of the bone shafts (**b**);

● the shapes, always curved to a greater or lesser degree;

59 MUSCLES OF THE HINDLEG OF THE HORSE CONCENTRATED IN FUNCTIONAL GROUPS (SIMPLIFIED)

To understand the leg properly as a constructed form, it is almost essential when drawing to leave out individual muscles and how they combine into complex masses.

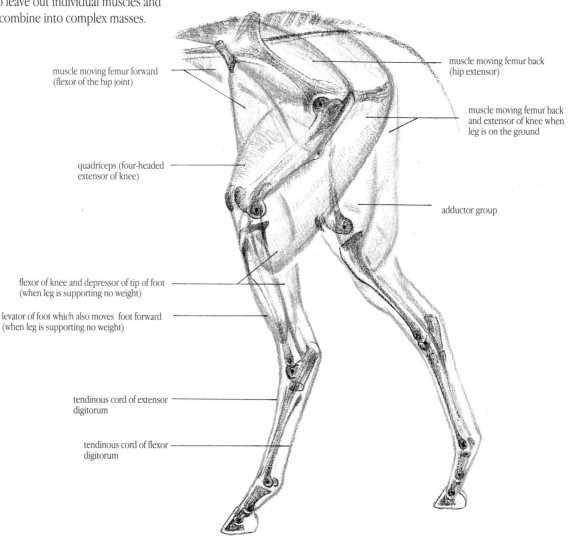

muscle moving femur forward (flexor of the hip joint)

muscle moving femur back (hip extensor)

muscle moving femur back and extensor of knee when leg is on the ground

quadriceps (four-headed extensor of knee)

adductor group

flexor of knee and depressor of tip of foot (when leg is supporting no weight)

levator of foot which also moves foot forward (when leg is supporting no weight)

tendinous cord of extensor digitorum

tendinous cord of flexor digitorum

- clarification of the visible planes and their three-dimensional distortions;
- cross-sections given as a guide to modeling;
- subordination of the subsidiary forms to the main ones;
- careful constructional treatment of the joints and the form of the foot, preparing for detail studies (c).

On the skeleton of the leg of a carnivore (fig. 58) note:
- the light construction of curved sections of the limb;
- the vertical position of the iliac wings, which are directed upward and forward;
- the way the foot is set down on the ground at the end of the metatarsus;
- the convex vaulting of the metatarsus on the upper side, its scooped-out concavity on the sole;
- the position of the digits: the different position of the phalanges in the dog and the lion needs to be worked out – a stepped drop of the phalanges in the dog because it does not have retractable claws, and the roof-like indentation of the phalanges in the cat with its retractable claws.

The above observations are intended as a preparation for understanding the leg musculature, with the muscles grouped into formal complexes. When considering the framework forms we largely ignore their subsidiary forms as details, in order to make the *formal connections* stand out all the more clearly (cf. fig. 54); the important thing to grasp is the links in the whole that take the pressure. With this in mind we look for the crucial, correlated points where the links of the chain connect. Making these continuous connections crystal clear is part of the task of creating order which is foremost for the graphic artist.

5.2
The musculature

If we are to understand the living form as a structural dialogue between hard, fixed skeletal forms and soft, variable muscle forms, we must give priority to the framework considered constructionally and functionally. So all that need be said about the leg muscles for present purposes is this: a muscle's mode of operation depends on where it crosses the joint axes between its point of origin and its insertion: if it passes in front of the cross-axes it is generally used for *extension*, if it passes behind for *flexion* (other functions are omitted). This means (see fig. 59):
- Muscles at the front in the space between the pelvis and femur move the femur forward, i.e. are *flexors* of the hip joint.
- Muscles in the rear part of the pelvis and the sacrum pass *behind* the cross-axis of the hip and femuro-tibial joint to the tibia. They are *extensors* of the hip joint and – since they cover two joints – *flexors* of the femuro-tibial joint (commonly called rump muscles).

- Muscles that emerge from the *front of* the pelvic area and the femur and extend in front of the cross-axis of the femuro-tibial joint to the tibia (passing by the patella) are *extensors* of the knee (e.g. a four-headed muscle known as the quadriceps).

If the leg is placed on the ground the rump muscles operate as bracing forces pushing forward. If the leg is bearing no weight they propel the femur and consequently the whole leg backward.

Groups of muscles with a position and function in front of and behind the cross-axis of the *tarsal joint*:
- The muscles that are in the front exterior area of the tibia, so passing over the front of the tarsal joint and down to the metatarsus or in some cases the digit (as in the horse), are *levator* muscles for the foot and *extensor* muscles for the digit.
- The muscles that occupy the space between the femur and the tibia on the side of the patella and go down to the calcaneum (by means of the powerful Achilles tendon) are *flexors* of the femuro-tibial joint and *depressors* of the tip of the foot, operating through the tarsal joint.
- Tendinous cords (activated by muscles located high up at the femur and tibia) to the rear of the metatarsus and the digits are *flexors* of the digital joints.

Wherever functional systems are illustrated in this book, the reader is asked to remember that information is given in very general and simplified terms. We here touch on a leading theme of this book, that of the basic skeletal structure which differs from one animal form to another, truly a theme with many variations. For example, the cow and carnivores have no real rump muscles, as the flexors of the knee start from the ischial tuberosities, not up at the sacrum. It would be possible to cite other differences between genera relating to the presence or absence of muscles in different forms of the foot. There is however one factor relating to the *distribution of muscle masses* which is common to all animals. Those that are arranged at the front or back of the cross-axes are the crucial driving forces of locomotive movement. This means that the flexor-extensor volumes lie on the front or back contour of the leg. *This in turn flattens the animal leg between the two sides* – in contrast to the human leg.

Moreover, the *bulk of the musculature is always located near the trunk*, i.e. it is always nearer the upper pivotal points than the lower ones. Thus the mass formed by the buttock muscles which direct the hip joint is in the pelvic area, the four heads of the knee extensor are nearer the femur than the knee, the rump muscles are nearer the hip joint than the femuro-tibial joint, etc.

To put it another way, there is basically a *continuous decrease in muscle mass as we move toward the periphery* (unloading). So that they can be fully effective, the joints are not laden with muscle mass. In an extreme example the joints at the end of the horse's leg are controlled by means of long, taut tendons.

60 FIRST PHASE IN THE LAYOUT OF
THE LIVING HINDLEG (HORSE)

The point of the assignment is to mark
the reference points of the skeleton
(shown in red shading) and show the
directions of the sections of the leg
unambiguously. It is preferable to use
straight contour lines to encourage the
use of concise accents. The different
planes, even very small ones, are also
indicated.

Pencil on A paper

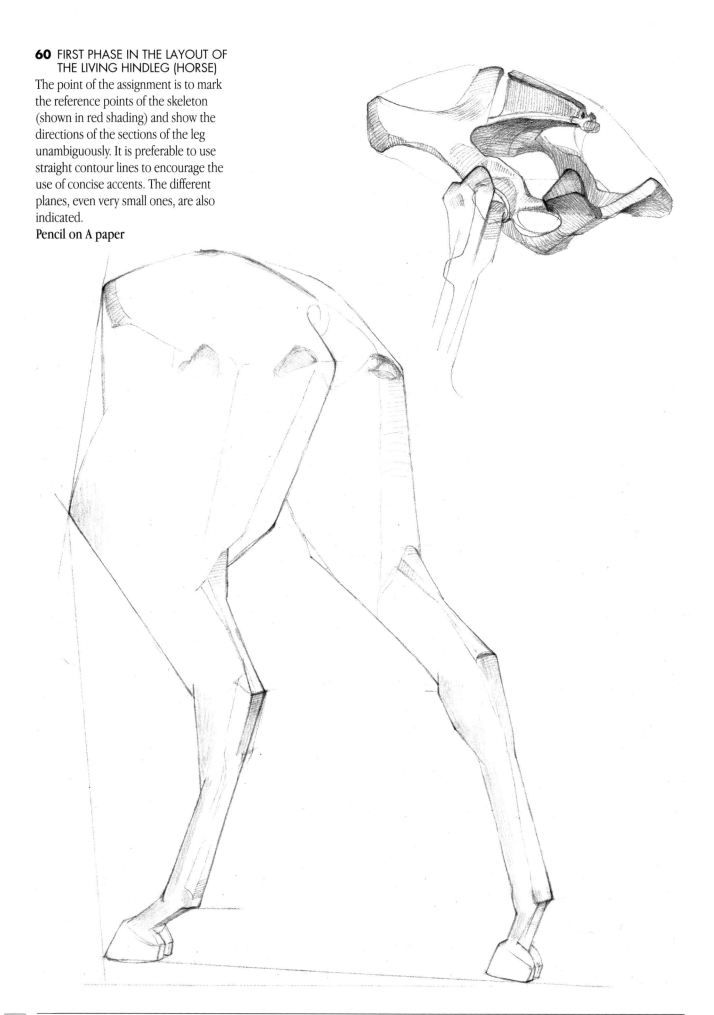

Section 5.2
The musculature

61 ENHANCING THE SOLIDITY OF
THE LIVING HINDLEG

To avoid swamping the drawing with too
much detail, an attempt is made to
emphasize the convergence of large,
important planes. The masses are so
constructed that a structural and
sculpturally convincing order can be
created from them.

Pencil on A3-size paper

5.3
Studies based on a constructional approach and on visualization

The construction of the skeleton and the disposition of the muscle system have been taken as guidelines for the understanding of the body's forms. We now bring these two topics together in some practical work, first turning to an exploration of the structural interplay between forms. The approach adopted in fig. 59 has already set us in this direction. The next sequence of examples continues and we shall then move on to a new level, testing the ability to retain and adapt knowledge in studies based on visualization. Strictly construction-based forms which do not encourage superficiality or effects for effect's sake come first. After this strict training and self-discipline we shall find the free, relaxed approach to forms in studies based on visualization all the easier.

62 MIXED MEDIA BRUSH STUDIES (ZEBU)
The quickly sketched forms produced with a small bristle brush and diluted Indian ink are followed by detail studies using a combination of pen, Indian ink and pencil to insert further details.
Indian ink, bristle brush, pen and pencil on A3-size paper

Section 5.3
Studies based on a constructional approach and on visualization

63 MOVING FROM INTENSIVE
OBSERVATION TO FLUENT LINE

Intensive treatment of what can be seen
(a) – here the hindlegs of a panther –
gradually develops into an increasingly
free linear record (b).

a

b

What are the primary considerations in drawing with a constructional concept of form (fig. 60)?

- First look for the points of reference that relate to the skeleton and join them together to see the shape they make.
- Thus, do not start off by thinking of the outline shape. This would all too easily degenerate into copy drawing of the outer appearance (losing all feeling for structure).
- Using the marks you have made, develop the viewing angle to the body, the planes that form the roof-like top cover of the body (space between the sacrum, sacral tuberosity, great trochanter and the ischial tuberosity) and the planes visible at the sides: outside, inside and rear.
- This basic approach should be adhered to even when dealing with small or slender forms like those of the tibia and foot.
- The basic forms and their main three-dimensional gradients should be set down in this way using straight lines. Curves should be avoided for the time being as they can detract from the succinctness of the form.

A block-like, relatively unfaceted image will emerge, an abstract creation ready for further development. It can then be enhanced (figs 11, 60) by:

- Elaborating the hollows and three-dimensionality of the body.
- Using hatching which can suggest the different angles of the planes quite clearly. The facets that emerge show where the forms meet with maximum contrast.
- Drawing in lines where the cross sections would run, which encourages thinking 'in the round' and helps organize the hatched areas to establish the spatial gradients.

Painterly effects using light and shade are alien to construction-based studies of this kind which depend on their underlying concept for their power to convince the observer that form has been understood. They represent a *distillation of form*, concisely encompassed in three-dimensional and solid organization. Careful, non-naturalistic studies of form such as these very soon engender new ways of looking and ideas of execution which may seem to leave the basics that have been assimilated behind, but in fact continue them and raise them to a higher level (figs 62, 63):

- The drawing should be constructed using a small, full, flat brush which forces you to set down only the most important constructional aspects of form and paves the way to discovering abbreviated ways of conveying form.
- A pencil or crayon is good for conveying massed groups of forms in their different sizes, and rounded, straight and convex shapes contrasting with powerful or gentle curves and firm forms.
- Once these skills have been mastered it is only a short step to recording with fluency.

Now we come to what I see as the most important outcome for artists of all anatomical study: the ability to work *from the imagination* productively and creatively, the act of expressing an accumulated store of perception, experience and knowledge in drawings from the *visual imagination*. The example we shall choose to illustrate this is a bucking horse (fig. 64). What general expectations can we have of such an exercise?

- A solid working study fit for its purpose, which is reliable, convincing and can be constructed and developed in its most important aspects;
- The achievement of thinking through an assignment and recognizing essentials.
- Intrinsic harmony of the whole.

The following principles are of prime importance:

- Harmony of proportions and unity of formal language.
- The contribution of structural and/or dynamic components.
- The integration of functions, heightening and exaggerating them.
- Clarity as to the viewing angle and the three-dimensional situation.
- Reduction of forms to elements as a working aid.
- The nature and sequence of intersections, foreshortenings and three-dimensional organization.

What working method is to be recommended for coming to terms with this type of project (fig. 64)?

- Simplifying (reducing to elements) the trunk-neck-head and limbs (a, b), then linking the cylindrical and four-sided shapes to one another.
- Establishing their spatial directions and the direction of any movement.
- Only then introducing any differentiation (c).
- Adding further anatomical factors (fig. 65), especially joints and free modeling masses.

The ability to create form and movement should be constantly retested using different media (figs 66, 67) or reversing the viewing angle.

Developing powers of visualization and imagination – quite apart from other subjective factors such as responsiveness, ability to see combinations and associations, sympathetic insight, abstraction, analysis, etc. – is emphatically *not* outside the realm of teaching and methodology. Visualization is one of the most important means of welding together all forces and ensuring their smooth and harmonious collaboration.

64 PRELIMINARY DRAWINGS LEADING UP TO WORK FROM IMAGINATION ALONE
It would be a sad loss if pictorial imagination and ideas were ever only directed toward depicting things that can be directly seen. That is why we mobilize our store of acquired knowledge and 'run it' in front of our mental eye. The power to visualize then proves its worth. This is the act of looking reproduced, prompted by aids in the shape of simplified forms.

Section 5.3
Studies based on a constructional approach and on visualization

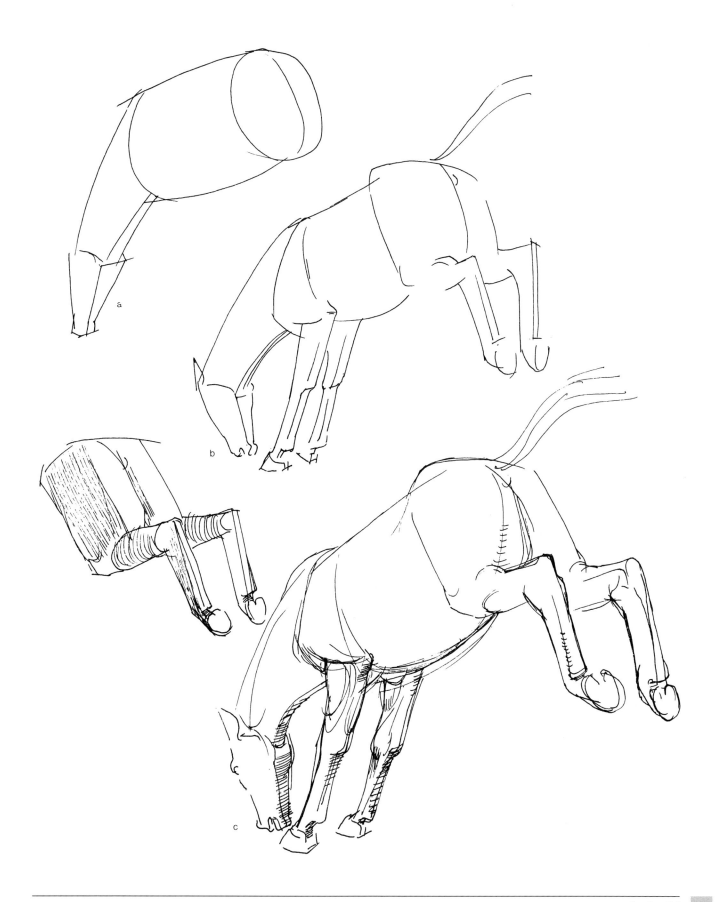

a

b

c

65 DRAWING FROM
        IMAGINATION: A FRESH START

Once basic factors such as the expression
of movement, the three-dimensional
situation and proportion (fig. 64) have
been worked out and are familiar, work
from imagination turns back to the
interplay of organic forms, which are now
both differentiated and enhanced. Here
we show students what can be done on
the theme of the bucking horse.

Pen and Indian ink on A4-size paper

Section 5.3
Studies based on a constructional approach and on visualization

66 CONSTRUCTING A DRAWING
FROM IMAGINATION USING
SKILLS AND EXPERIENCE
ACQUIRED

Reverting to the technical experience
gained in studies with a brush, a further
check is made on imaginative capability.
We see the bucking horse in the same
gesture as in figs 64 and 65, but now at an
altered viewing angle and imagined from
a different point of view (three-quarter
front view).
**Watercolor and flat watercolor brush on
A4-size paper**

67 AN EVEN FREER APPROACH
Another variation on our theme, with a
different viewpoint and type of horse.
The drawing is executed in a gently
exploratory manner, and the 'sharpness
of movement' emphasizes the theme still
more.
**Watercolor crayon, diluted with plain
water in places, on A3-size paper**

Section 5.3
Studies based on a constructional approach and on visualization

6.

The forms of the foreleg

Again the construction of the skeleton of the limb can be explained with reference to the animal's way of life. As the shoulder does not have to provide thrust, it can take on more differentiated and varied tasks, again specific to the species in question; we shall therefore deal separately with the types of construction found in animals adapted to running, carnivores and primates. Any forelimb that has to make gripping movements during climbing or hanging has different constructional requirements.

Cats with their ability to climb must be able to use their paws to cling to trunks and branches. This means a freer use of the arm in general, as well as the ability to turn the paw as a result of the ability of the radius to turn round the ulna. In animals that are specialized runners, *ungulates*, there is no need for this functional ability or the construction that goes with it. *Primates* on the other hand have an astonishing range of arm and hand movement in every direction. As well as the ability of the shoulder girdle and shoulder joint to move freely in every direction, there is the *hand's ability to grip*. The unit incorporating the shoulder and foreleg has become an all-purpose instrument in primates. In spite of constructional and functional differences between animal types in the way in which the front limb is used, there are some common features:

- the number and sequence of the joints,
- the directions followed by sections of the limbs,
- the positions of the joints in relation to the trunk, especially the shoulder and elbow joints,
- the disposition of the musculature in relation to the joint axes.

6.1
Drawing the shoulder and foreleg of specialized runners (fig. 68)

Animals in which the sole functions of the shoulder and foreleg are to support the weight of the front of the body and transmit the thrust conveyed by the rear limbs are what we mean by specialized runners. Let us first consider the skeletal structure of ungulates.

- They have an *undivided shoulder girdle* (scapula) which is the basis of the pendulum movement of the free-swinging shoulder and foreleg mass. It is not fixed like the pelvis, but can move beyond the thorax in a backward and forward direction.
- The angle between the scapula and humerus is open to the

back. At the pivotal point (*shoulder joint*) the humerus reaches forward by means of extension, and backward by means of flexion, so that the whole limb mass is capable of a forward-backward swing.

- The scapula is flexibly suspended on muscle straps (fig. 6). This makes it possible for the trunk to have spring suspension during walking, running and jumping. There is no clavicle.
- The shoulder girdle and humerus nestle in close to the steep side of the thorax, which helps the pendulum movement and virtually directly supports the body's center of gravity.
- The front limbs are positioned in the middle of the frontal body mass – two-thirds of the total body mass (almost at the point of equilibrium of the head, neck and thorax).
- The radius is fused with the ulna, and forms a straight line with the carpal joint and metacarpus (saving muscle energy).
- The tendons are non-fatigable and the elbow joint can be fixed (a snap joint).
- All joints other than the shoulder joint are purely hinging joints to safeguard the dominating flexing and extending movements.
- The metacarpal bones are elongated like stilts, prolonging the leg pendulum.
- The end members of the digits are made of a hard-wearing horny material adapted for standing and walking on the tips of the toes.

The shoulder girdle
In specialized runners the shoulder girdle consists of only the scapula, the part least affected in all animal forms by adaptation specific to the species. It is a triangular bone with rounded-off or pointed corners, pointing down and forward as it gets narrower, and containing the socket of the shoulder joint. The spine running down the scapula indicates its slanting position even on the living animal.

The forearm and carpal joint
These are the essential factors for drawing purposes:
- The carpus of the hand or foot is always jointed on to the radius (as in humans).
- For ungulates that are purely specialized runners the radius's ability to turn the foot would be more of a hindrance than a help so, as we have seen, the radius and ulna are fused together.
- The radius supports the weight of the front of the body; the 'back of the hand' is pointing forward (pronation position) and is wider than it is deep.
- The carpus complex makes flexion and extension possible in the carpal joint. When flexed the metacarpal bones disengage into two superimposed rows. This gives rise to the wide, flat shape of the carpal joint (at the carpus it is therefore a sliding joint).

Metacarpus and first digital joint
- The weight of the body of perissodactyls is offloaded onto one powerful metacarpal bone.
- At the bottom and back of the metacarpus are two sesamoid bones which account for the thickened shape above the fetlock.

- The roller at the end of the metacarpus has a sharp-edged guiding ridge (see the side drawing in fig. 68) to ensure the hinging movement in flexing and extending.
- The subsequent joints are constructed on the same, very close-fitting principle.
- The end member of the digits is protected in a horn shoe.

Distinctive plastic features of the shoulder and foreleg of a specialized runner in profile
The plastic features of the skeleton are easier to recognize in the foreleg than the hindleg – the following stand out:
- The continuous modeling of the scapula, especially at the upper edge near the withers, with the spine of the scapula clearly visible. The sloping angle of the scapula is evident.
- There is almost a right angle between the scapula and humerus which presses through the pectoral muscles at the front of the chest to form the point of the shoulder joint (foremost point for measuring the length of the trunk) which serves as a ledge on which a horse collar can rest.
- The end of the muscle-clad humerus is indirectly indicated by the sharply projecting ulna.
- The skeleton of the forearm becomes bare of muscles only at the level of the carpal joint on the outside and at front, while the inside of the radius is uncovered for its entire length.
- At the rear to the side where the carpus starts the pisiform juts out, providing the profile of the living leg with a heel leading into the metacarpus.
- The shape of the foot is determined by the skeleton, except for flexor tendons which stand out prominently on the flexing side.
- The backward-pointing sesamoid bones above the first digital joint cause a nodular swelling in the form at the foot.

The skeleton of the foreleg in front view
- The wide step-like shoulder girdle stands out clearly from the neck.
- The inside of the radius above the knee joint is emphasized by a sharply projecting bulge.
- The carpus is very wide.
- The forearm characteristically slants inwards.

68 STEP-BY-STEP WORKING STUDY OF THE SHOULDER AND FORELEG OF THE HORSE
a) The directional lines of the sections of the limb are established with the length of each.
b) Three-quarter front view emphasizing the series of joint axes and shapes. Red shading: formal components determining the modeling of the living leg.
c) Detail study of the shape of the elbow joint: the fusion of the ulna and radius in specialized runners has resulted in this becoming a pure hinge joint.

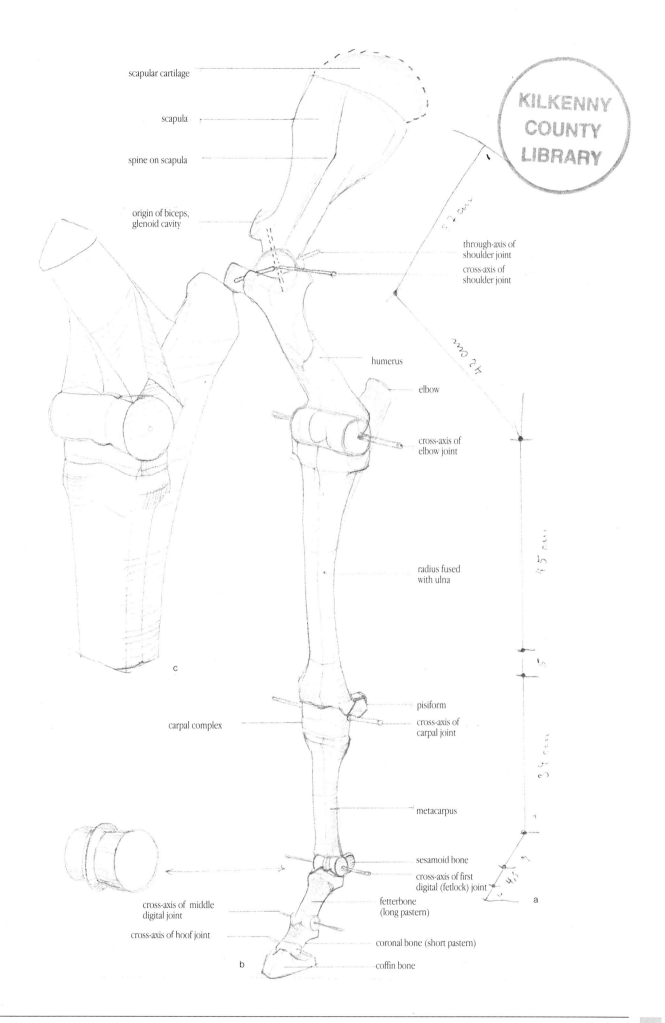

scapular cartilage

scapula

spine on scapula

origin of biceps,
glenoid cavity

through-axis of
shoulder joint

cross-axis of
shoulder joint

humerus

elbow

cross-axis of
elbow joint

radius fused
with ulna

c

pisiform

cross-axis of
carpal joint

carpal complex

metacarpus

sesamoid bone

cross-axis of first
digital (fetlock) joint

cross-axis of middle
digital joint

fetterbone
(long pastern)

cross-axis of hoof joint

coronal bone (short pastern)

b

coffin bone

a

Graphic investigations of skeletal forms of the shoulder and foreleg (fig. 68)

- The lengths of the sections of the limb should be visually assessed (a).
- The directions of the sections should be established (a).
- Emphasis should be placed on the constructional forms (b, c), and care taken to draw in the lines followed by the joint axes and three-dimensional axes (based on viewing angle).
- It is important to make clear what is mechanically feasible,
- and to make sure no formal accents are omitted.
- Attention must be paid to curves in the sections of the skeleton (skeletal forms are neither rigid nor straight).

Impact of joint mechanics on form (fig. 69)

The flexible, mobile positioning of the scapula and the way in which it can stick out at the top mean that it is not a constant plastic shape:

- The humerus is brought forward by extending the shoulder joint, and moves back if it is flexed.
- When the carpal joint flexes, the two rows of bones disengage (fig. 69b). The way in which the metacarpus tucks under in a lying position produces an enlargement and blunting of the mass of the carpal joint.
- The reverse side of the flexed digital joints does not consist of a smooth curve, but of small arcs interrupted by articulation.

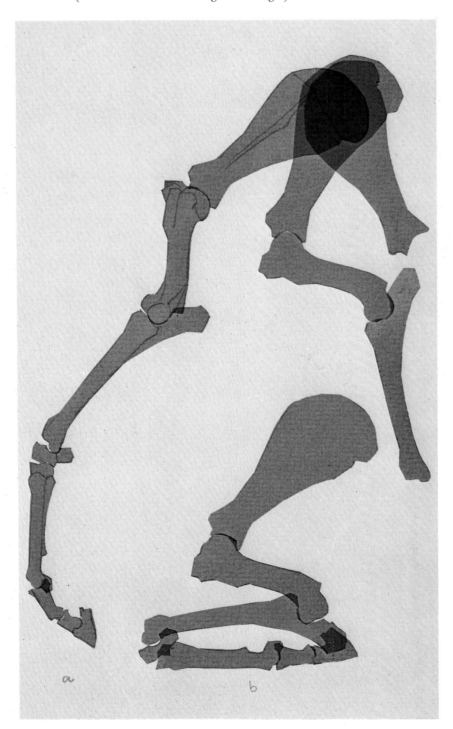

69 JOINT MECHANICS IN THE SHOULDER AND FORELEG OF A SPECIALIZED RUNNER (HORSE)

a) A slight shift in the position of the scapula (swinging it forward) prepares for a considerable swinging movement of the limb governing the use of the foot, which can be further affected by the combined effect of the other joints in the foreleg.

b) Angles of the joints in a closed position (passive flexing, e.g. when lying down).

6.2
Disposition of the musculature in specialized runners

As the freedom of movement of the peripheral joints is increasingly restricted, there is a corresponding diminution of muscle. Given that the muscles around the joints close to the trunk (shoulder joint and to some extent elbow joint) are generally the same in all animal forms, there are also more analogies in their disposition (fig. 70):

- Muscles from the skeleton of the trunk encompassing the shoulder girdle form the group of *trunk-shoulder-girdle*

muscles with the task of suspending the trunk between the scapulas (figs 25a, b) or suspending the limb from the spinal column when it is not bearing any weight.

- Muscles from the skeleton of the trunk encompassing the humerus and forearm are *trunk-limb muscles* with the task of swinging the limb forward and backward in animals that walk on the ground, and of performing hoisting movements in climbers (apes).

- The muscles acting on the limb itself are called *true limb muscles.*

The two first-mentioned groups of muscles are sometimes superficial and thin and sometimes concealed, so they are not discussed here.

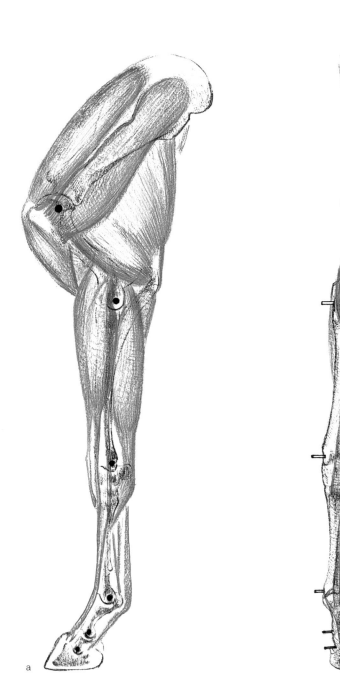

70 MUSCLES OF THE FORELEG OF THE HORSE GROUPED ACCORDING TO FUNCTION (SIMPLIFIED)

In order to understand the form of the leg as a constructional concept (see also fig. 59), you should omit detail studies of muscles and their complexes.

a) The profile view with the joint axes (black dots) and the associated muscle groups makes the rhythm of the shapes clear.

b) The front view, again with the cross-axes marked, shows how all muscle masses flatten off at the sides.

a

b

The group of true limb muscles in specialized runners
These are situated with reference to the moving joint axes (figs 68, 70) which govern the functions (fig. 70):

- Muscles occupying the space in front of the spine of the scapula and consequently lying in front of the cross-axis of the shoulder joint and inserted at the humerus operate *extension*, so moving the humerus forward.
- The space behind the spine of the scapula in the open angle between the scapula and humerus is occupied by *flexors* lying behind the cross-axis of the shoulder joint.
- The three-part *extensor* of the elbow joint (the triceps) operates simultaneously in this area: it lies behind the cross-axis of the elbow joint.
- The front space between the humerus and forearm is occupied by *flexors* lying in front of the cross-axis of the elbow joint.
- The layer of muscles lying in front of the leg in the area above the elbow joint traveling in front of its cross-axis and down to the carpal joint and digital joints has a double function: *flexion* at the elbow joint and *extension* at the joints below.
- Muscles lying at the back of the forearm and foot may even pass over the cross-axes of the elbow, knee and digital joints, acting as *flexors* of the latter two.

In terms of plasticity this disposition has the following effects (figs 70a, b):

- The flexors and extensors layered one behind the other invariably create a deep mass, i.e. in their spread from the front of the leg to the back (a), while the front view (b) from side to side is very much flattened off.
- The lower limb has a covering of muscles at the front and on the outside, *never* on the inside of the leg.
- From just above the carpal joint the modeling of the skeleton is dominant as the peripheral joints have only long, taut tendons passing over them.

These focal points are the basis of our graphic treatment of the foreleg of specialized runners.

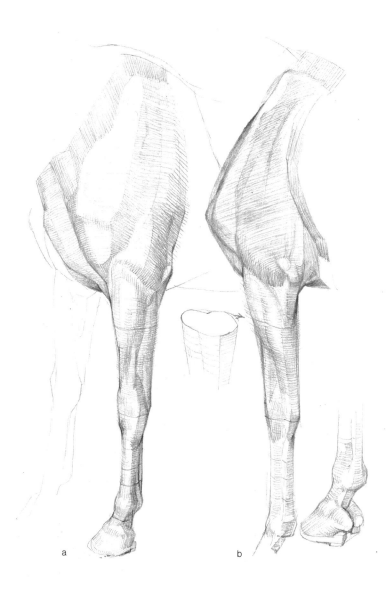

a   b

71 USE OF A CONSTRUCTIONAL DRAWING TO STUDY THE FORM OF THE SHOULDER AND FORELEG OF A LIVING ANIMAL
The shoulder girdle is elaborated as a flat, triangular attachment to the side of the thorax and standing out clearly from the start of the neck at its side. Study of the free leg is supported by indicating the alternating muscle and skeletal masses.
Pencil on A4-size paper

Section 6.2
Disposition of the musculature in specialized runners

6.3
The whole leg of a runner: constructional analysis and drawing from imagination

The suggestions made as regards the hindleg again apply here, and further criteria should be borne in mind:

- In modeling, the position of the triangle in the shoulder area should be based on the direction of the spine on the scapula.
- The narrow shape of the scapula – running from the upper shoulder, standing out from the rest of the body and becoming increasingly prominent as it reaches the shoulder joint – must be worked out (fig. 71a).
- The shape of the side of the shoulder girdle should be brought together to form a triangle.
- The shoulder joint should be made to stand out well at the front as a clearly projecting curve.

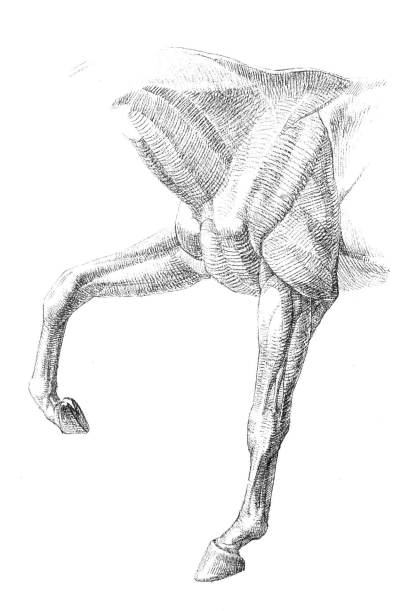

72 ARCHITECTURAL DRAWING OF THE SHOULDER AND FORELEG

If a structural drawing is not based on analytical understanding of the skeletal and muscle structures (see figs. 68, 70) any drawing attempt will result in a muddle. In the learning process a structural drawing is an intermediate stage, opening up the way to many forms of artistic representation, to an abstract shorthand depiction of form, and various decorative and monumental approaches.

Black chalk on A3-size paper

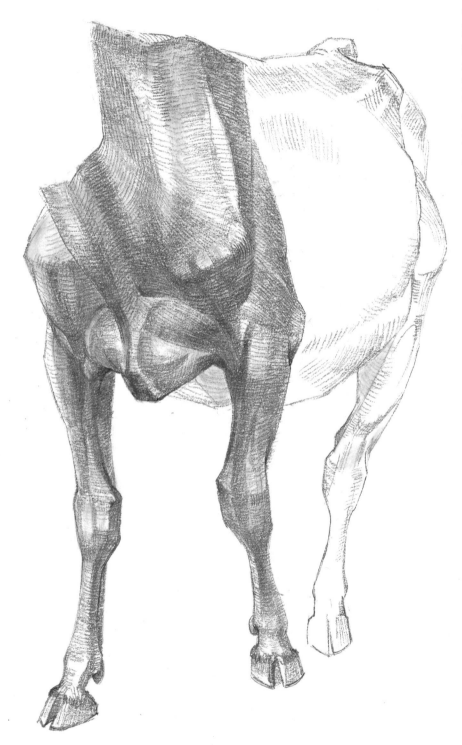

73 TYPICAL FORM OF A COW'S LEG
In comparison with the horse the shapes of the muscles and bones of the cow, particularly their most prominent features, are harder and more angular. Attention should be paid in particular to the great width of the carpal joint and the bend above and below it.

74 ANALYTICAL KNOWLEDGE AND FREEDOM OF EXECUTION COMBINING IN A UNIFIED WHOLE (NILGAI ANTELOPE)
When working freely from life, knowledge of the rules governing anatomical form and its modifications must have become second nature, so that you need to glance at the real, continually moving animal only occasionally to provide the essential finishing touches.
Watercolor crayon, pen, brush and watercolor on A3-size drawing paper

Section 6.2
The whole leg of a runner: constructional analysis and drawing from imagination

nilganantilope

g.B.
84

The whole leg of a runner: constructional analysis and drawing from imagination

- The pronounced cone shape of the forearm – flattened at the sides – should be worked out and clarified with cross-sections.
- Note the contrast between the dimensions of the forearm and those of the cross-section of the carpal joint.
- The difference between the metacarpus, again deeper than it is wide, and the dimensions of the carpal joint should be made clear.
- The bulging strands of the flexor tendons should appear taut and rigid (fig. 71b).
- The slenderness of the first phalanx should be clearly contrasted with the swelling above the hoof.
- The angularity of the elbow should be accentuated, not smoothed off.

The shoulder and foreleg of the cow (fig. 73) are generally more angular than those of the horse, and the carpal joint is extremely broad. But above all emphasis must be placed on the bend between the upper leg and metacarpus: this is generally far more pronounced in ruminants (fig. 73) than in horses.

Drawing from nature is not an opportunity to display erudition, but rather a combination of a visual experience and the application of knowledge, an attempt to interpret. A master such as Leonardo da Vinci was always trying to ensure his artistic work was 'correct' by carrying out special detail studies and continually endeavoring to extend his repertory of forms (fig. 76). What would become of the most marvelous ideas for pictures if in creating them artists could not draw on all they have stored in their imagination? Rethel was not in a position to observe how Phrygians broke in horses (fig. 77), and Picasso did not have to rush off to an arena to sketch a bull attacking a toppled horse (fig. 78). Visual experience and the ability to visualize underpin and guarantee the discovery of convincing organic form. Without these the poetry of moving form will not be imparted.

The leg of a specialized runner: drawing from imagination
In further exercises from imagination (fig. 80):
- We can test what has been – and has not yet been – understood.
- We want to avoid producing work where muscle structure and forms have been only half assimilated, so reinforcing the seeing habits associated with them.
- We want to give equal weight to empathy, feeling and the power to conjure up images, alongside pure study from nature.
- If in so doing we touch on areas not yet tackled, we should not be daunted.

Because we want to stimulate imaginative activity we shall not move on immediately to a set theme where forms are reduced to elements. Our preliminary attempt takes the following form (fig. 80):
- Take your widest watercolor brush generously filled with diluted paint and make carefree, sweeping, energetic strokes across the paper with it – make a real mark.
- You should have no set shape or predetermined concept in mind.

- Let the marks run and arrange themselves and take your inspiration from them.
- Only then should you take a pen and ink and follow whatever shapes your marks may suggest, for instance the curve of a bent neck.

Make a necessity of chance. The pen will be helpful as the work takes on more definition: let the creative idea flow from your pen. It is important to repeat such experiments again and again. Deriving pleasure from play takes its place alongside a strict search for form.

We now return to that search, exploring the theme of a collapsing horse (figs 79a, b – 84):
- Start by using basic blocked shapes for all parts and show how the angular shoulder girdle nestles into the barrel shape of the trunk (fig. 81).
- It is important to be totally concrete regarding solidity and three-dimensionality.
- Experiment to see how the gesture you have in mind works out most expressively.
- Rather than being satisfied with your first attempt, improve on it with a graphic texture (fig. 82).
- Vary the theme, exaggerating the gesture, starting all over again with forms reduced to elements (fig. 83).
- If you think you have found an expressive gesture and a clear, functionally convincing solution, be daring and try it out on a larger, more ambitious scale conceived more as a full-scale picture (fig. 84).

Continuing to work freely in this way with fluid and more precise media, heightening the gesture into angularity, dislocation and even tragedy, will make you aware of how great a store of imagination you can call on and explore, and how inexhaustible it is.

Section 6.2
The whole leg of a runner: constructional analysis and drawing from imagination

75 EXPLORATORY CHARACTER OF AN ARTISTIC STUDY

The rising interest in reality and curiosity toward nature in the Italian early Renaissance engendered the abundance of analytic detailed observations such as that recorded here on expensive parchment.

Antonio Pisanello (1395 - c. 1455), Cow, facing left, rising from a lying to a standing position.

Silver point (worked over with a brush?) on parchment, 7 x 9 in (17 x 23.1 cm), Paris, Louvre

76 ELEVATING A NATURAL THING TO THE ROLE OF ARTISTIC SUBJECT

Given new and greater value by the artist with his deep insight into nature and its laws, the familiar horse's leg becomes the object of artistic curiosity.

Leonardo da Vinci (1452-1519), A horse's foreleg in different positions.

Drawing, Windsor, Royal Library

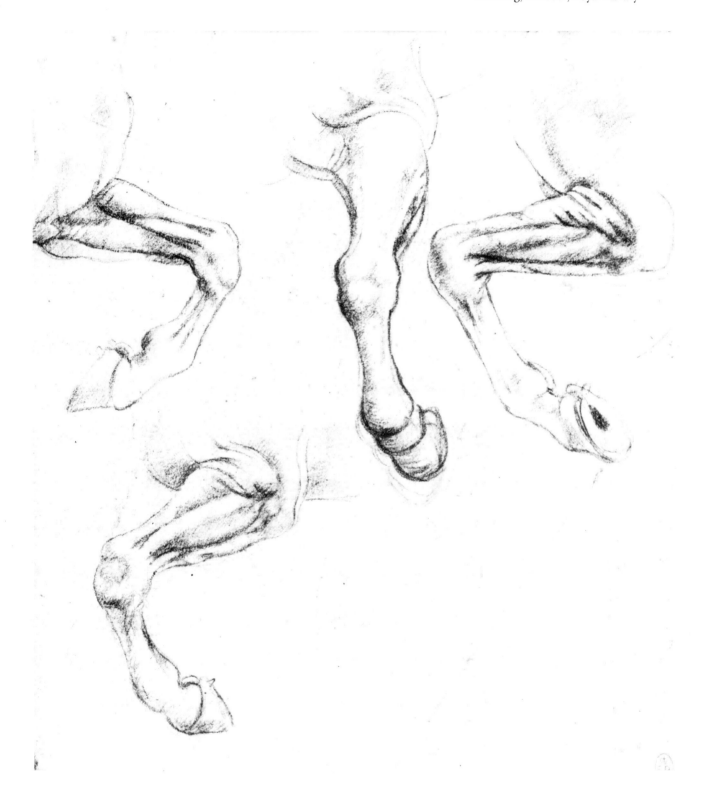

77 ARTISTIC USE OF VISUALIZED NATURAL FORMS IN A PICTORIAL CONCEPT

An artist's idea for a picture cannot always rely on the availability of a model from life. Rethel, who belonged to the Romantic school and was a master of its attractive forms, has transformed imagined but believable natural figures into severe, clear-cut, monumental forms. Alfred Rethel (1816-59), Strength (Phrygians breaking in a horse).
Dresden, Kupferstichkabinett (print room)

78 THE INDIVISIBILITY OF PERSONAL EXPERIENCE, EXPERIENCE OF NATURE AND VISUAL EXPERIENCE

Two animal figures, two species, each in an appropriate gesture, texture and form, drawn with classic linearity in a single rhythmic flow that has its origin in the maturity derived from observation. Pablo Picasso (1881-1973), Bull and horse, 1927.
Etching, 7½ x 11 in (19.2 x 27.9 cm)

Section 6.2
The whole leg of a runner: constructional analysis and drawing from imagination

79a SKETCH OF AN INITIAL IDEA
FOR A SET THEME:
COLLAPSING HORSE

The pen or pencil reacts seismo-graphically to the ebb and flow of the imagination. Whether such drawings are clumsy or skillful, appealing or unappealing, is not the point of the exercise. This uncorrected example highlights the way in which the masses are brought out in enveloping curves.
Pen and Indian ink on A4-size paper

79b DRAMATIZING THE GESTURE BY
REINFORCING THE CONTRASTS

The theme and the formal solution do not yet match up convincingly, so further attempts are made to convey the subject better; the broader contrasts do not resolve the problem satisfactorily, still giving too strong an impression that the horse is running away.
Monotype on glass, approximately A3-size

80 MAKING MARKS AS A WAY OF STIMULATING IMAGINATIVE POWER

Making colored marks on paper in a random way can give rise to all sorts of shapes which can be exploited as a preliminary to free invention. A few bold curves drawn in with a pen and Indian ink can enable a mark to crystallize into the figure aimed for, backed up by one or two curving strokes with the brush: the result is a horse rearing.

Watercolor and pen on A4-size paper

81 CLARIFYING FORMS BY REDUCING THEM TO ELEMENTS: A PREPARATORY STAGE FOR A DRAWING FROM IMAGINATION

Form should not be elucidated by starting with an outline, but by indicating the basic volumes. These build up into a formal structure which calls on knowledge of anatomy, which is used to supply the building blocks of work based on visualization.

Pencil on A4-size paper

82 ENHANCING A THEMATIC ASSIGNMENT BY USING A TEXTURE BASED ON RANDOM MARKS

Even the smudges printed from the fantastic textures of a monotype can give rise to ideas that inspire the artist to draw a collapsing horse into them with a pen. However, it is open to question whether the gesture of collapsing has been convincingly conveyed.

Pen and Indian ink drawing on blot textures in acrylic paint printed as a monotype, A4-size paper

Section 6.2
The whole leg of a runner: constructional analysis and drawing from imagination

83 WORKING STUDY FOR A NEW
CONCEPT OF THE THEME OF
THE COLLAPSING HORSE

The new concept – inspired by the fact
that the gesture had still not been
convincingly conveyed – introduces a
configuration of highly expressive
components which highlight what is
happening functionally.

Pencil on A4-size paper

84 FINISHED VERSION OF THE
INITIAL SKETCH

Between fig. 81 and this picture there is a
division of work in which the discovery of
the form is transferred to the working
study, so that points of emphasis can be
reinforced in the finished drawing. Color
is applied to give contrast and pen to
indicate articulation.

**Pen on wet watercolor paint, A4-size
paper**

6.4
Drawing the shoulder and foreleg of carnivores

As has already been said, the shoulder girdle is the area that varies least from the general structural design, and this applies to the cat family too, as far down as the elbow joint. The crucial variation here relates to the independently formed, unfused ulna and the radius that can move round it, providing pronounced supination and pronation in cats – though it is very restricted in dogs. This ability requires the radius to cross the ulna to a greater or lesser degree as it travels down toward the foot, which results in cats having a broad carpal joint, while dogs have a narrower one (figs 86b, f). The following specific functional demands are made by the carnivores' way of life (fig. 86):

- Sideways movement (abduction) of the humerus in the shoulder joint of cats (climbing, attack).
- Ability of cats – which can climb – to turn the paw.
- When the paw is placed on the ground the rear of the paw faces forward (pronation position (fig. 86e, h).
- In profile the paws of dogs and cats differ in their direction: the dog's paw bends slightly forward after the carpal joint (figs 86a, d), while the cat's is straighter (figs 83e, h).
- In front view the cat's paw is more angular in the forearm

section (fig. 86f) than that of the dog which pursues its prey (fig. 86b).

The paw of a carnivore displays very different features from the foot of an ungulate (fig. 86):

- A fan-like five-rayed metacarpus (only four rays at the back).
- Existence of a pollex or thumb at the top of the paw, which has a functional purpose only in cats (spread of the paw).
- Development of the phalanges into claws, retractable in the cat, non-retractable in the dog.
- The weight of the body is supported on the extremities of the metacarpus, hence the existence of pressure-distributing pads on the digits.
- The metacarpus curves clearly both lengthwise and transversally (short digital muscles are located in this area).

Using constructional simplifications in the ulna and radius and the metacarpus, we once again illustrate the shared and diverging features of form in the skeletons of the foreleg of the horse, lion and ape: it is especially important to note how the radius and ulna twist round one another in carnivores and primates. Yet again the formal connections are emphasized (as in fig. 83), in line with the criteria previously recommended for studies of the skeleton.

The course of the pivotal axis in the forearm of the lion is marked with a red dotted line in fig. 88a, b, c to help you understand the bone structure with its striking functional and plastic impact.

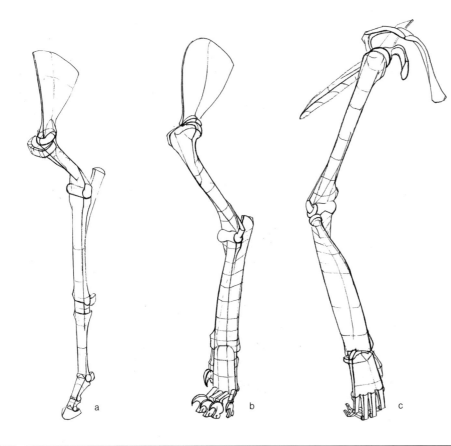

85 THREE DIFFERENT TYPES OF CONSTRUCTION IN THE SHOULDER AND FORELEG

a) Specialized runner (horse)
b) Carnivore (lion)
c) Brachiating animal (ape)
The forearms of the carnivore and the brachiating animal are represented as helically twisted complexes, although the ulna and radius are in fact fully independently formed. The paw or hand is attached almost exclusively to the radius.

86 SKELETON OF THE LEFT SHOULDER AND FORELEG OF CARNIVORES

Top row: dog; bottom row, lion. The constructional differences between these and specialized runners are very evident in the construction of the forearm and the paw. Here the ulna and radius exist as two separate, fully developed single bones. The radius crosses the ulna so that the rear of the paw faces front (pronation position). The foot is five-rayed.
a, e) External profile
b, f) Front view
c, g) Back view
d, h) Internal profile

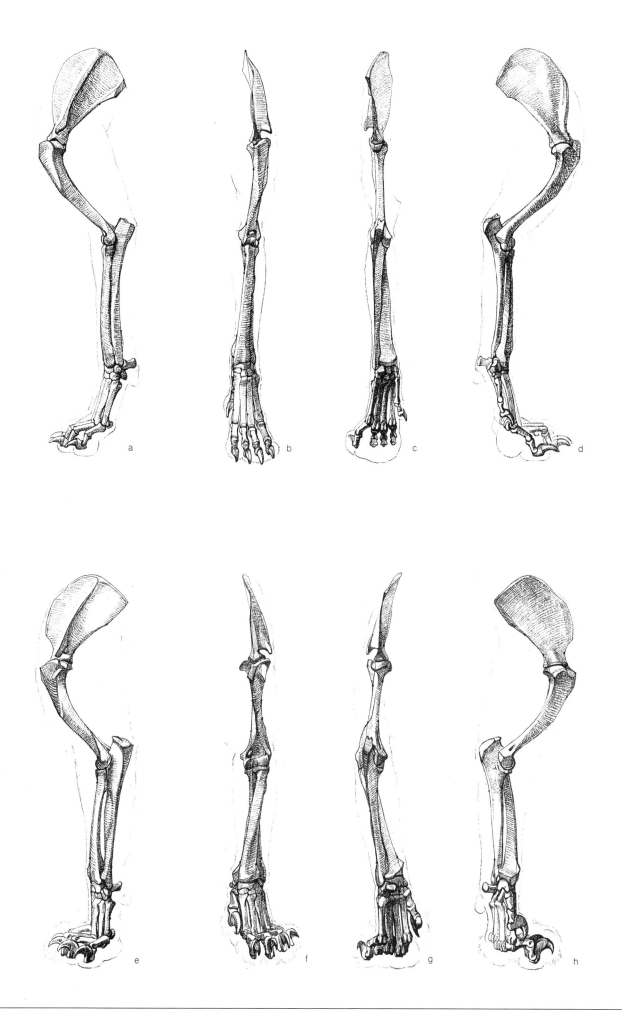

87 WORKING STEPS IN GRAPHIC STUDIES OF THE SKELETON OF SHOULDER AND FORELEG OF A DOG

a) Investigating the relative lengths and directions of skeletal sections in front view.

b) Finished study of the basic factors (in a)).

c) Detail of the foot with the directions of the digits, three-quarter external view.

d) Detail of a claw.

e) Three-quarter front view.

f) Internal view.

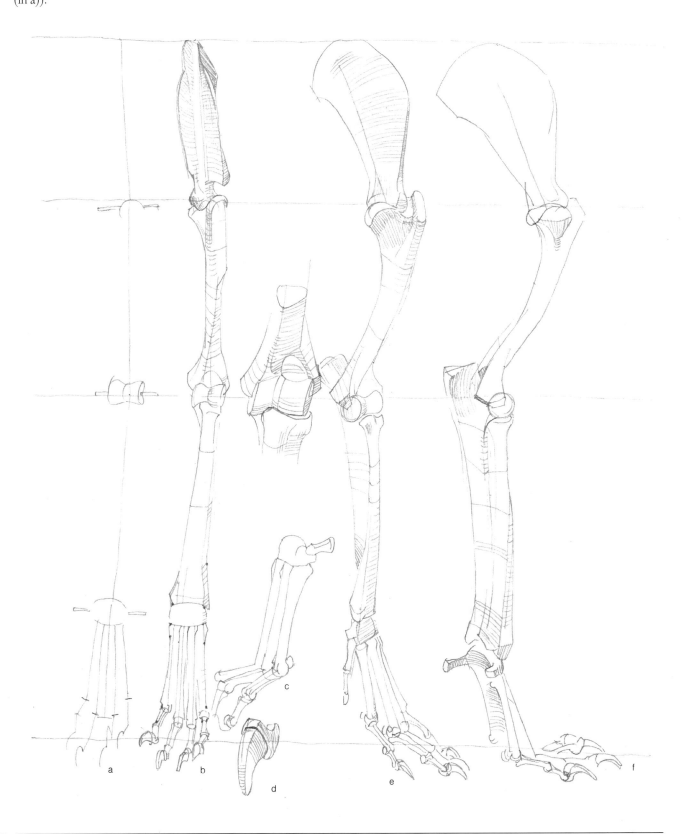

Section 6.4
Drawing the shoulder and foreleg of carnivores

88 STUDY OF THE SKELETON OF SHOULDER AND FORELEG OF A LION, EMPHASIZING THREE-DIMENSIONALITY AND CONDENSING FORMS

An essential of this study is to explore how organic forms penetrate space when distorted in several ways. Here again the capacity of the bones of the lower limb to change position merits special attention.

a, b) Right forearm showing the pivotal axis of the radius turning round the ulna.
c) Door-hinge principle in the forearm where a 'wing' (the radius) swivels round the longitudinal axis.
d) Shape of a lion's thorax.
Model study drawn by the author at a Bammes course at the Schule für Gestaltung, Zurich

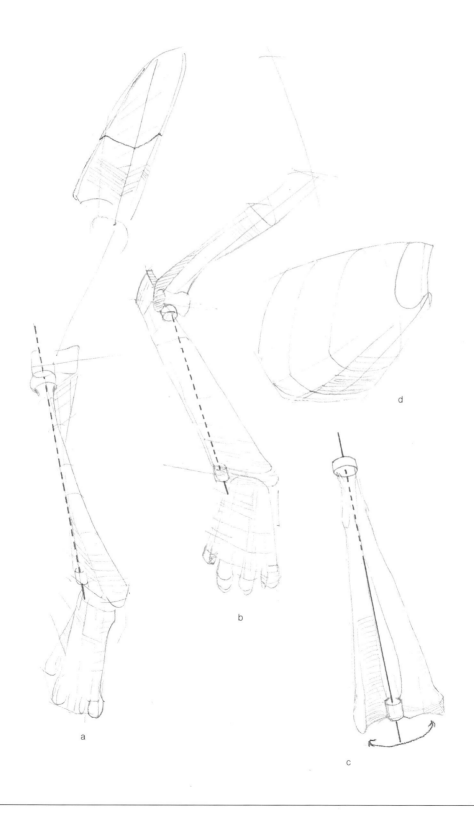

a

b

c

d

6.5
Basic disposition of the musculature

The same criteria as before apply for understanding the disposition of the functional groups of muscles. However, in the cat family the position of the foot in relation to the ground and its extremely varied functional uses have resulted in the lower part of the limb having a powerful muscle covering – in contrast to ungulates – in order to operate the carpal joint and the phalanges (fig. 89). The *extensors* of the carpal joint pass in front of its cross-axis, originating on the lowest external section of the

humerus and being inserted to the base near the carpus at the back of the metacarpus (fig. 92a). The *flexors* on the other hand are behind the cross-axis, originating on the lowermost inside section of the humerus and being inserted at the base of the hollow side of the metacarpus (fig. 92b).

The flexion group is the more massive because of the great and versatile use of the paw, and its importance to survival. To underline the athletic, compact form of the shoulder and forearm of the lion (fig. 89) as a hunter that lies in wait, we also depict those of the dog to demonstrate the light build of the hunter that pursues its prey (fig. 90).

89 MUSCLES IN THE SHOULDER AND FORELEG OF A CARNIVORE (LION, SIMPLIFIED)
The modus operandi of individual foreleg muscles assembled into functional groups and scapula and humerus muscles can be deduced from their position in relation to the joint axes (black dots, and at the carpal joint three-dimensionally drawn axes).

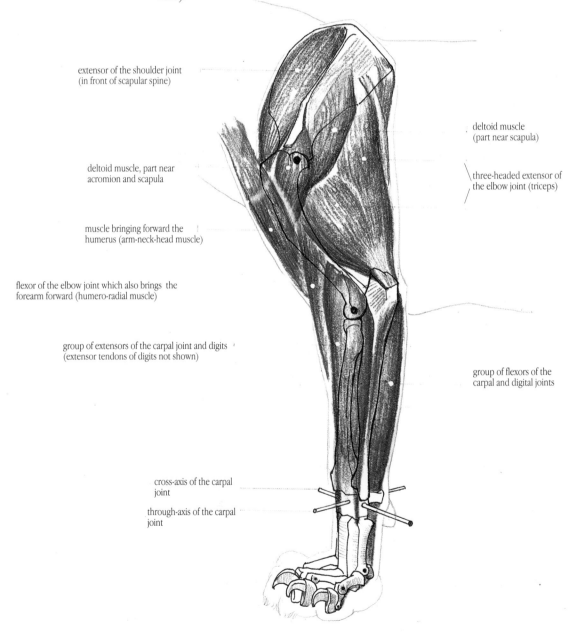

extensor of the shoulder joint
(in front of scapular spine)

deltoid muscle
(part near scapula)

deltoid muscle, part near
acromion and scapula

three-headed extensor of
the elbow joint (triceps)

muscle bringing forward the
humerus (arm-neck-head muscle)

flexor of the elbow joint which also brings the
forearm forward (humero-radial muscle)

group of extensors of the carpal joint and digits
(extensor tendons of digits not shown)

group of flexors of the
carpal and digital joints

cross-axis of the carpal
joint

through-axis of the carpal
joint

90 MUSCLES IN THE SHOULDER
AND FORELEG OF THE DOG
As in all other mammals the muscles that
operate on the carpal joint and the digital
joints (in red) are arranged with the cone
of the muscle near the pivotal point
nearest to the trunk.

91 MUSCLES IN THE SHOULDER
AND FORELEG OF THE COW
As in fig. 90 the muscles in the forearm
are shown in red; in contrast to those of
the carnivore they travel down to the
digits in very long tendons, thus allowing
the skeletal shape to make the dominant
impression.

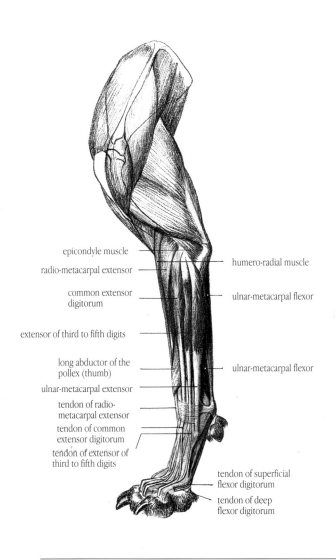

epicondyle muscle

radio-metacarpal extensor

common extensor
digitorum

extensor of third to fifth digits

long abductor of the
pollex (thumb)

ulnar-metacarpal extensor

tendon of radio-
metacarpal extensor

tendon of common
extensor digitorum

tendon of extensor of
third to fifth digits

humero-radial muscle

ulnar-metacarpal flexor

ulnar-metacarpal flexor

tendon of superficial
flexor digitorum

tendon of deep
flexor digitorum

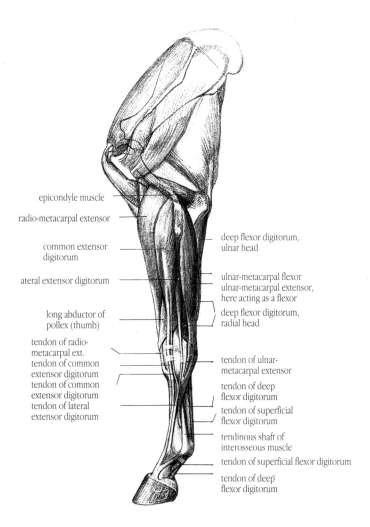

epicondyle muscle

radio-metacarpal extensor

common extensor
digitorum

ateral extensor digitorum

long abductor of
pollex (thumb)

tendon of radio-
metacarpal ext.
tendon of common
extensor digitorum
tendon of common
extensor digitorum
tendon of lateral
extensor digitorum

deep flexor digitorum,
ulnar head

ulnar-metacarpal flexor
ulnar-metacarpal extensor,
here acting as a flexor
deep flexor digitorum,
radial head

tendon of ulnar-
metacarpal extensor

tendon of deep
flexor digitorum

tendon of superficial
flexor digitorum

tendinous shaft of
interosseous muscle

tendon of superficial flexor digitorum

tendon of deep
flexor digitorum

92 PRINCIPLES OF THE ARRANGEMENT OF MUSCLES IN THE FOREARM OF A LION

To make it easier to understand how the muscles are arranged to operate the carpal and digital joints, the directions they follow are indicated in colored bands. These show:

a) front view with skeletal forms,
b) back view with skeletal forms.
The flexors have a greater mass than the extensors.

c) Abstract illustration of origin and insertion points, without any indication of the skeleton of the forearm. The flexors (red) originate at the internal epicondyle of the humerus, while the extensors (blue) originate at the external epicondyle of the humerus, and they are inserted on the back and front (hollow) sides of the bottom of the metacarpus respectively.

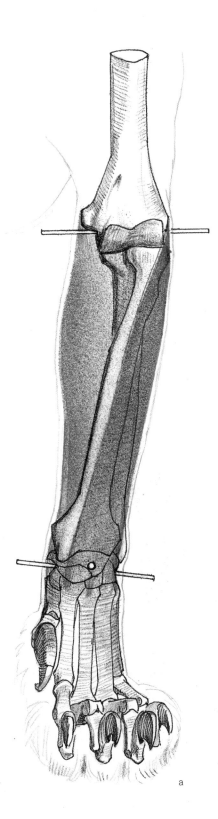

a

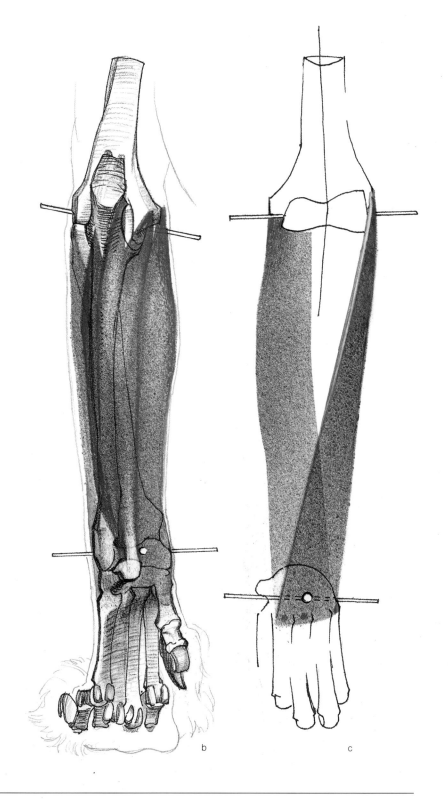

b

c

Section 6.5
Basic disposition of the musculature

93 FRONT PAWS OF TWO CARNIVORES
a) Lion's paw.
b) Dog's paw.
The illustration emphasizes the stubby shape of the lion's paw, and the graceful shape of the dog's, the former with a short metacarpal construction and the retractable claws, the latter with a long metacarpal construction and non-retractable claws.

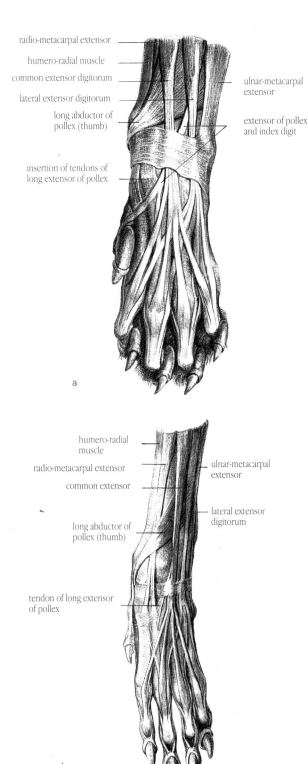

radio-metacarpal extensor

humero-radial muscle

common extensor digitorum

lateral extensor digitorum

long abductor of pollex (thumb)

ulnar-metacarpal extensor

extensor of pollex and index digit

insertion of tendons of long extensor of pollex

a

humero-radial muscle

radio-metacarpal extensor

common extensor

ulnar-metacarpal extensor

lateral extensor digitorum

long abductor of pollex (thumb)

tendon of long extensor of pollex

b

6.6
A constructional approach combined with visualization

Patient observation and much repetition are now required to embark on the fairly slow process of building up an informed repertoire. The following principles should be borne in mind (figs 94, 95):

- It is important to grasp the main muscle masses (fig. 94) and follow them, however restless the animal's movements may be. The movements and views that recur most often are the typical ones.

- Attention should be paid to the sharpness of any skeletal protuberances.

- The basics of the skeletal form should always be explored by drawing in peace and quiet at home after life studies at a zoo (fig. 94b).

- Bearing in mind what positions the forelimb and paw appear in most frequently, reduce what you have observed to the simplest, blocked shapes (fig. 94c).

- The position of the pollex (thumb) on the inside of the paw and the way in which the forearm and metacarpus positions correspond because of the radius's ability to turn (figs 94, 95, 96) must also be explored.

Drawing from imagination
Here again we shall use a set theme, and the lack of an actual animal as a model should be no cause for complaint: its very absence often leads to a quicker, readier grasp of the essential. Using the example of a big cat crouching and stretching, (fig. 97):

- Go through the same steps as in figs 80, 81, 82 and 83, and sketch in the taut curve of the cylinder formed by the trunk (fig. 97a).

- Bring the shoulders and forelegs including the scapula forward in an expressive way (fig. 97b).

- Show the hindlegs folded down ready to spring, paying attention to the dimensions of the body's masses.

- The shoulders and forelegs should be treated in the same way, bringing out the distortion in the forearm (width of the paw placed on the ground).

- In the cat that is stretching, indicate how the lumbar region forms a concave bend with the chest section (fig. 97c).

- Show the forelegs splayed out wide apart, with the claws out and the metacarpus spreading out like a fan.

- Spatial recession should be heightened by exaggerating the real volume of the forearm and paw.

- The eyes should be drowsily closed, no threatening gesture (mouth closed).

- In conveying solidity ensure that the small shoulder area nestles tight against the steep side of the thorax, while the forearm spreads out like a fan right down to the paw.

Once these fundamentals have been assimilated the student can begin on a picture, always provided the preliminary work is done thoroughly (fig. 98).

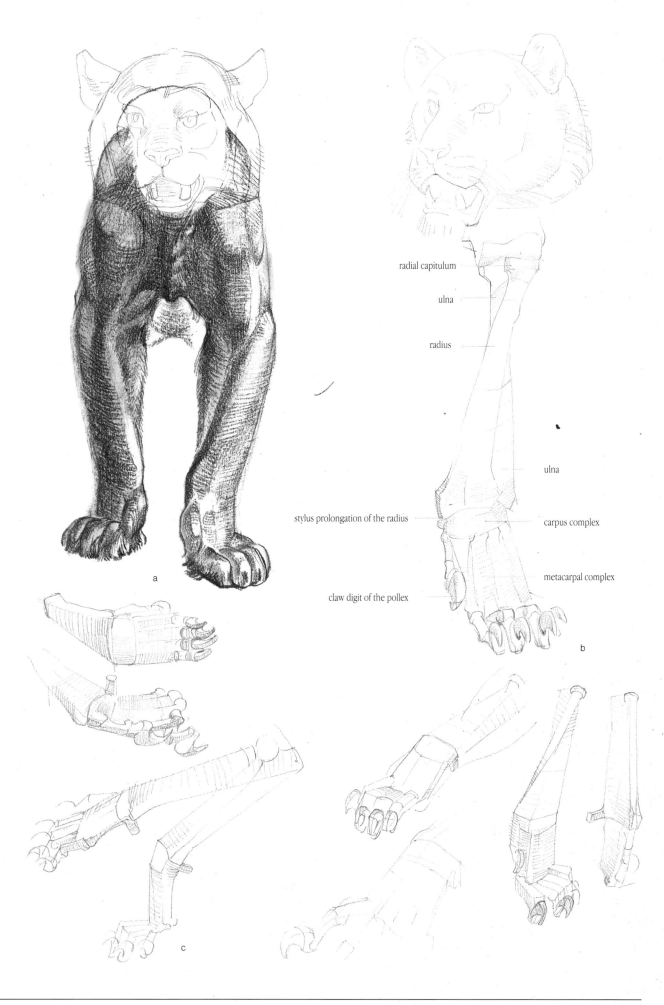

radial capitulum

ulna

radius

ulna

stylus prolongation of the radius

carpus complex

metacarpal complex

claw digit of the pollex

a

b

c

Section 6.6
A constructional approach combined with visualization

94 THE IMPACT OF THE MUSCLES ON THE MODELING OF THE SHOULDERS AND FORELEGS OF A TIGER; THE VARIOUS WAYS IN WHICH THE PAW IS HELD AND PLACED

a) The diagonal direction of the radius can also be seen as a line separating extensor and flexor muscles. Although it is covered with fur the paw is an articulated mass.

b) Skeleton of the left forearm of the lion in the pronation position (back of the paw facing forward).

c) Variations in the paw position mainly showing supination, pronation, flexion and extension.

95 STUDIES FROM LIFE OF A JAGUAR, CONCENTRATING ON THE PLASTIC BEHAVIOR OF THE SHOULDERS AND FORELIMBS

Careful drawing finds the expression of the scapula in a standing, weight-bearing position and the attitude of the paw where the carpal joint is bent producing inward-turning supination. The paw stretched out in front is in a pronation position (back of the paw facing upward).

96a PAWS IN VARIOUS POSITIONS
Top right: lion's paw in pronation.
Bottom left: jaguar's paw in pronation
with foreshortening from the front, and a
paw in an intermediate position between
supination and pronation.

96b STUDIES OF THE JAGUAR FROM
LIFE
A prime consideration in these studies is
the shape and attitude of paws held in
different ways.

Section 6.6
A constructional approach combined with visualization

97 VISUAL STUDIES OF TWO
CONTRASTING POSES: A BIG
CAT CROUCHED AGGRESSIVELY,
AND STRETCHING

The psychological and functional
expression is once again centered on
formulating the behavior of trunk and
head.

a) Overall tension of the trunk. The
practical knowledge now attained is
exploited in a working study of the idea.
Formal stability comes from simplification
and the juxtaposition of clear planar
directions.
b) The drawing of the gesture with the
emphasis on the behavior of the limbs
bears the same considerations in mind.
c) The gesture of stretching – note the
hollow curve formed by the vertebral
column.

25.3.84
g.Bo.

To free up what has been established in the idea sketch it is often useful to change to different, more responsive media.
Red chalk and watercolor paint on colored paper

99 SPECIAL FORM OF THE SHOULDER AND FORELIMB OF THE APE

a) Directions of the skeleton of the arm with the external angles and the crossed position of the radius (pronation).
b) Total turning axis of the arm from the shoulder joint down to and including the radio-ulnar joints enabling the radius to turn, along with the axes of other individual joints.
c) Left arm, with the various joint axes that serve to control the use of the hand drawn in, starting with the internal clavicular joint.
d, e) Skeleton of the forearm and metacarpus shown diagrammatically, together with the way in which the radius turns at the proximal and distal radio-ulnar joints.

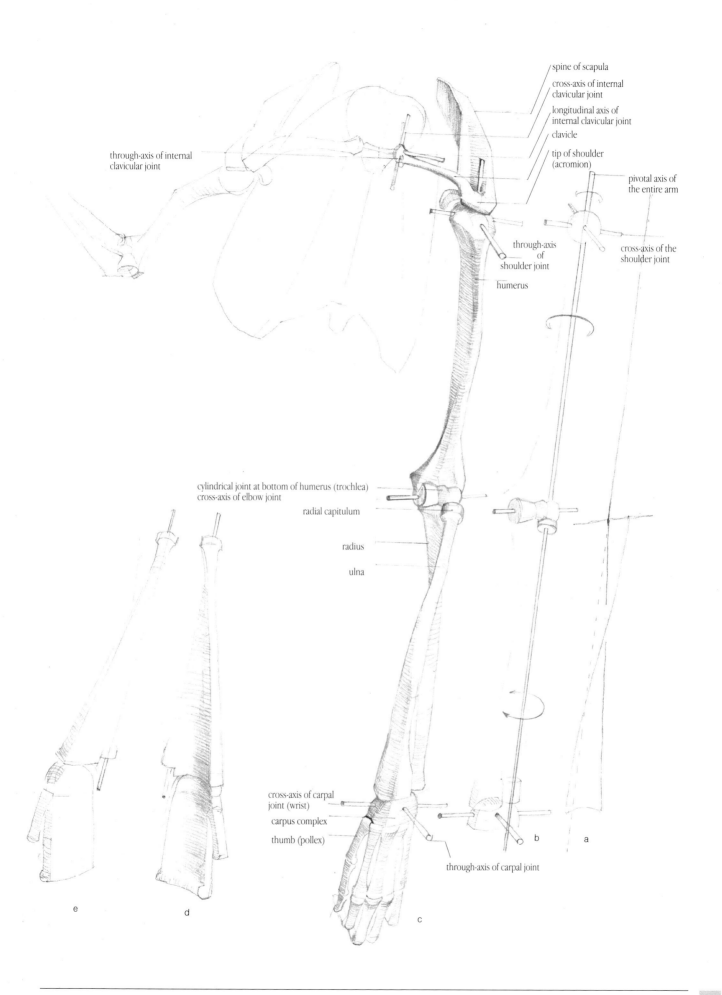

spine of scapula

cross-axis of internal clavicular joint

longitudinal axis of internal clavicular joint

clavicle

tip of shoulder (acromion)

through-axis of internal clavicular joint

pivotal axis of the entire arm

through-axis of shoulder joint

cross-axis of the shoulder joint

humerus

cylindrical joint at bottom of humerus (trochlea)
cross-axis of elbow joint

radial capitulum

radius

ulna

cross-axis of carpal joint (wrist)

carpus complex

thumb (pollex)

through-axis of carpal joint

e

d

c

b

a

6.7
The special shape of the shoulder girdle in primates

Many of the factors we are already familiar with through looking at the shoulder and foreleg of carnivores are repeated in primates, but there are further, unique factors enabling primates to swing, hang and move from tree to tree (fig. 99):

- The two-part nature of the shoulder girdle (scapula and clavicle).
- The perfect, combined elbow joint with the *radius's capacity to turn* round a common pivotal axis of the entire arm (b) using the superbly developed proximal and distal radio-ulnar joints.
- The ellipsoidal carpal joint (wrist) that can move at two levels with flexion, extension and abduction toward the thumb and the little finger.
- The existence of a *hand* rather than a paw, with a *thumb* that can move of its own accord to join fingers which are themselves able to move independently.

The versatility of the hand is the result of the combined operation of all the constructional factors in the skeleton of the arm:

- The mobile two-part shoulder girdle is the effective base for versatile use of the arm.
- The clavicle serves to brace the arm away from the thorax.
- Subtly differentiated use of the hand is produced by *six* joints:
  the internal clavicle joint,
  the external clavicle joint,
  the shoulder joint (ball and socket joint with three basic axes: swinging forward and back, sideways adduction and abduction, inward and outward rotation),
  the humero-ulnar (elbow) joint with a cross-axis for flexion and extension,
  the proximal and distal radio-ulnar joints working on a door-hinge principle for supination and pronation,
  and the ellipsoidal carpal (wrist) joint with cross-axis and abduction toward the thumb and the little finger.

This marvelous construction which is also present in human beings means that the hand can be used at any point within the cone described by the free arm. The hand's ability to grip as a result of the opposite position of the thumb means primates have a qualitatively unique and innovative instrument in comparison with the foot and the paw.

100 SHOULDER GIRDLE AND ARM
SKELETON OF A GORILLA

The scapula with its extensive surface (dark shading) is the extremely mobile base of the arm and an appropriate, practical necessity for climbing and hanging. Compared with man, the scapula is further to the side of the thorax which is virtually square in cross-section.

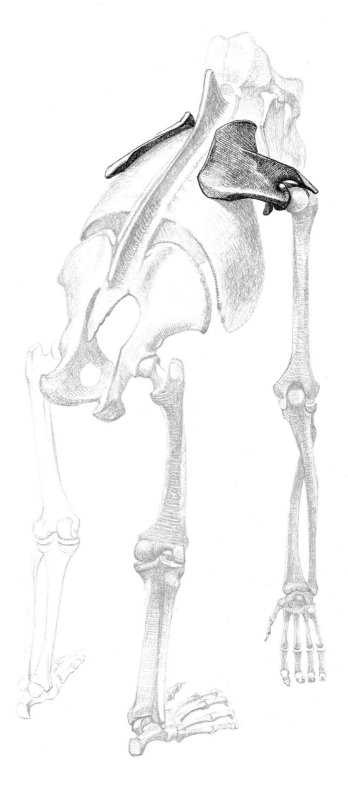

7.

The form of the trunk

In considering the trunk we again give pride of place to skeleton forms – the vertebral column, thorax and pelvis (the latter already touched on in connection with free suspension of the hindlegs). We shall not go into the subtleties of the precise anatomical construction of the vertebral column or thorax, but seek to assimilate their general appearance. As with the limbs, there are common factors in the structural design of the trunks of all species, but in the case of the trunk it is more important to bring out the specifics of each animal.

The *vertebral column*, perceived as the arch of a bridge, has no great mass, the important factors to bear in mind when drawing it are the partly concealed location of its moving points and its outline shape. The *thorax* is inevitably considered as the invisible plastic core, the *pure trunk muscles* completing, fastening and shaping the trunk between the pelvis and thorax. The *pelvis* can either be regarded as part of the trunk or along with the hindlegs. In Chapter 5 it was considered as the base for the free-swinging leg pendulum and as a link between the legs and the vertebral column.

7.1
Study of the vertebral column as a structure creating form

This marvel of function and construction:
- supports the weight of the internal organs of the chest and stomach;
- protects the central nerve tracts;
- facilitates the use of the directional sensory organs, particularly through its attachment to the head;
- plays a contributory role in respiration;
- plays a contributory role in locomotive movement through changes in its curvature;
- alters the spatial relationship between the pelvis and thorax.

It is divided into the following sections: cervical vertebrae (CV), thoracic (or dorsal) vertebrae (TV), lumbar vertebrae (LV) and caudal vertebrae (CAV). The different sections are capable of different movements:
- The CV section has the greatest all-round freedom of movement for holding and using the head.
- The TV section has the ability to move sideways and twist lengthwise (torsion). Limited flexion and extension.

- The LV section is capable of very limited lengthwise torsion.
- In the CAV section there is all-round unrestricted movement (in practical terms lengthwise torsion is not required).

Each vertebra consists of a body articulated with back-pointing spinous processes which vary in length from very long to very short and are linked together by ligaments; the points of these form the backbone, determining the specific, expressive back contour of each species of animal in repose and motion. *The course followed by the back contour, the line of the back, is one of the crucial vehicles of expression in animal form.* The extended crest of a range of mountains is what makes it impressive, and the spine of the course of the back has the same function in an animal. Let us consider a few examples (fig. 101):
- *Brown bear*: highest point is the sacrum, and from there the line bends forward in a long, shallow, C-shaped hump, and falls away sharply behind.
- *Gorilla*: highest point in the line of the back is close behind the head, which makes the head look pulled in. It then falls continuously down to the tip of the sacrum. The overall line of the back is a shallow C-shape.
- *Human being* (leaning forward on all fours): highest point where TV give way to LV (lumbar hump). A long curve slopes down to the back of the head which lies much lower than the sacrum. The overall line of the back is C-shaped, but in an upright attitude (fig. 101 bottom left, shown in an unnatural horizontal position) it is a double-S-shape.
- *Horse*: withers and croup are more or less on the same horizontal level. The line of the back at the withers forms a convex curve with a shallow fall to the LV, a shallow convex rise to the sacrum, then another shallow fall.
- *Cow*: the whole vertebral column climbs slightly toward the tip of the sacrum. At the transition from the TV to the LV there is a very shallow angle open toward the animal's back.
- *Big cat* (lion): horizontal line from the withers to the croup with a smooth transition from the TV to the LV. From the croup there is a shallow drop toward the tail.
- *Dog*: withers and croup on the same horizontal level. The line of the back between them forms a very obtuse angle open at the top.

The mechanics of the vertebral column in flexion and extension produce the following effects on form:
- When the neck and head are raised (extension) there is a marked curve at the point where the CV give way to the TV: neck-chest curve.
- The withers stand out when the neck is lowered (flexion).
- A bend occurs in the vertebral column where the TV give way to the LV when carnivores are sitting (lumbar hump), and a dip (extension) occurs in the suspension phase of jumping and when taking off (figs 42, 43).
- The lowering of the neck causes tension in the ligament connection between the withers and the head (flexible nuchal ligament), causing the spinal processes in the withers to straighten up and strengthen the shape of the back of the neck.

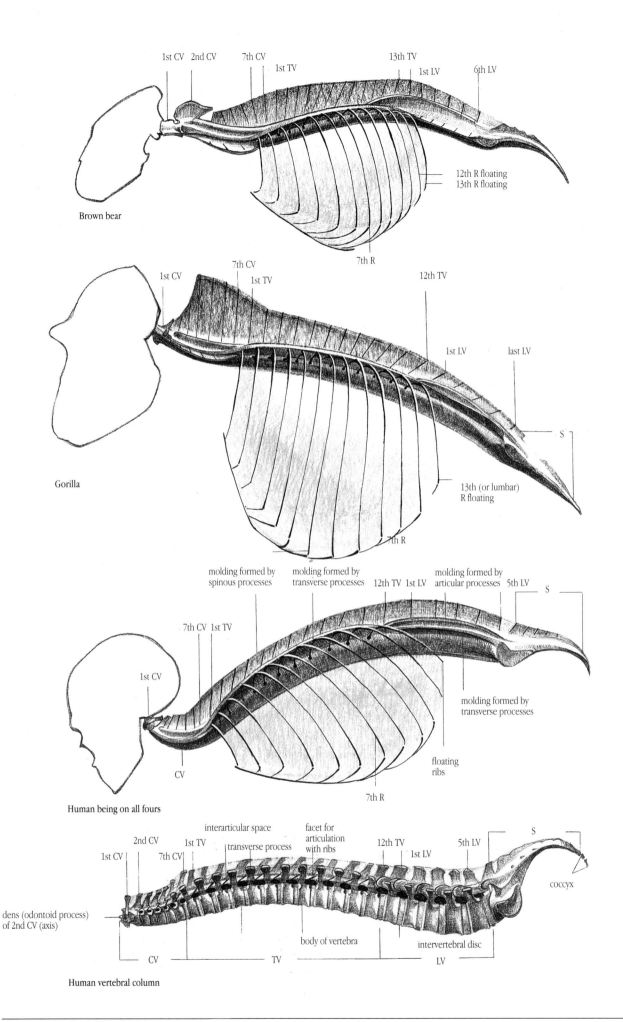

1st CV   2nd CV   7th CV   13th TV
                            1st TV   1st LV   6th LV

12th R floating
13th R floating

Brown bear

7th R

                7th CV
1st CV   1st TV   12th TV
                                                      1st LV   last LV

                                                                          S

Gorilla

13th (or lumbar)
R floating

7th R

molding formed by   molding formed by   molding formed by
spinous processes   transverse processes   12th TV 1st LV   articular processes   5th LV   S

        7th CV 1st TV
1st CV

                                                                          molding formed by
                                                                          transverse processes

        CV

                                                            floating
                                                            ribs

Human being on all fours   7th R

                                    interarticular space   facet for
                2nd CV   articulation
                        7th CV   1st TV   with ribs   12th TV   S
1st CV   transverse process   1st LV   5th LV

                                                                                        coccyx

dens (odontoid process)
of 2nd CV (axis)

                                                body of vertebra   intervertebral disc

        CV   TV   LV

Human vertebral column

Section 7.1
Studies of the vertebral column as a structure creating form

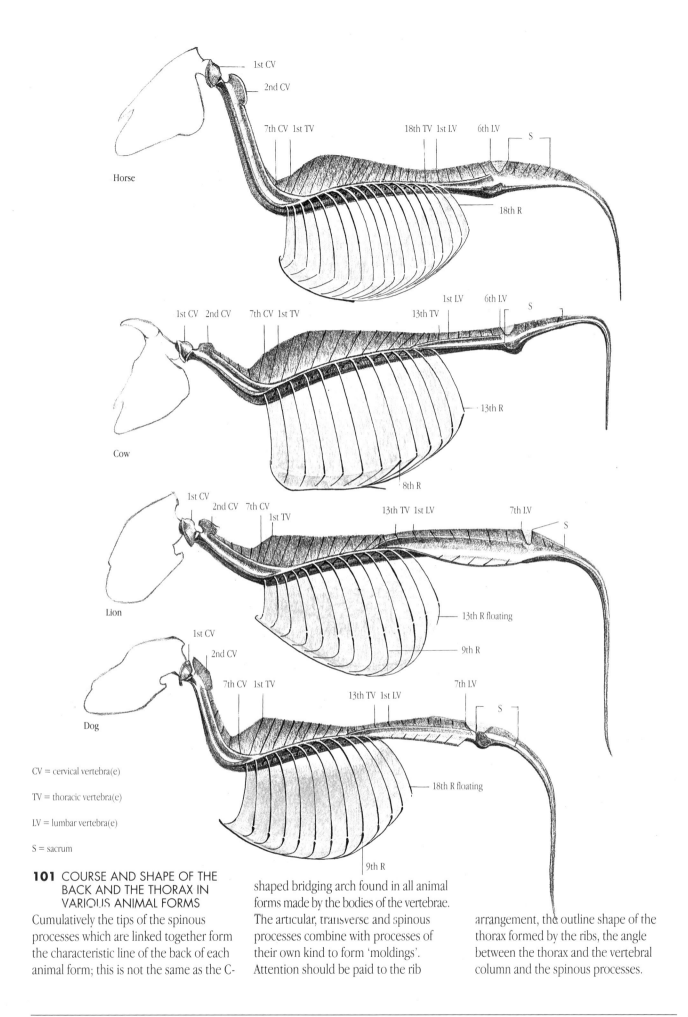

Horse

1st CV
2nd CV
7th CV 1st TV
18th TV 1st LV 6th LV S
18th R

Cow

1st CV 2nd CV 7th CV 1st TV
13th TV 1st LV 6th LV S
13th R
8th R

Lion

1st CV
2nd CV 7th CV
1st TV
13th TV 1st LV
7th LV S
13th R floating
9th R

Dog

1st CV
2nd CV
7th CV 1st TV
13th TV 1st LV
7th LV S
18th R floating
9th R

CV = cervical vertebra(e)

TV = thoracic vertebra(e)

LV = lumbar vertebra(e)

S = sacrum

101 COURSE AND SHAPE OF THE
BACK AND THE THORAX IN
VARIOUS ANIMAL FORMS

Cumulatively the tips of the spinous
processes which are linked together form
the characteristic line of the back of each
animal form; this is not the same as the C-
shaped bridging arch found in all animal
forms made by the bodies of the vertebrae.
The articular, transverse and spinous
processes combine with processes of
their own kind to form 'moldings'.
Attention should be paid to the rib
arrangement, the outline shape of the
thorax formed by the ribs, the angle
between the thorax and the vertebral
column and the spinous processes.

These simplified comments imply two important factors where studies of animals are concerned: the course of the line of the back is a vehicle for expressing movement and at the same time an indicator of the three-dimensional situation – the position of the central axis of the body in space. I would advise the following procedure:

- First judge the overall course of the direction of the vertebral column (clarifying the viewing angle), noting its rises and falls.
- The starting point should not be a detail or a 'cut-out' silhouette. The course of the central axis should be drawn without lifting your pen, in a single line running from the tip of the nose to the tip of the tail.
- Practice doing this until you are completely confident of direction, rises and falls, and relative lengths of each section.
- Constantly observe how much the overall expression changes with the alteration of the line of the back. Contour lines and internal forms should not be added until you are sure of the course and shape of the line of the back.
- This work should be done very fast, almost intuitively.

Only once these skills have been acquired can modeling be developed on a sound basis (fig. 106). When trying to work out what happens to form if the trunk is twisted (front of the body straight, thighs lying sideways), it is a good idea to get things clear by reducing forms to elements, imagining the trunk as a twisted four-sided mass (fig. 105). This method is also useful for solving similar problems in drawing from imagination.

If you cannot convey this two-dimensionally, shape a piece of Plasticine into a four-sided log with slightly rounded corners. Holding both ends, twist them carefully in opposite directions until you achieve the required torsion. In theory you should get a shape (fig. 105b-e) that is twisted like a propeller. *Simplifying things in this way is intended to make organic shapes transparently clear by means of uncomplicated, easy-to-do intermediate working stages, and to fix functional thinking in your mind through hands-on experimentation.*

102 THE IMPORTANCE OF THE COURSE OF THE VERTEBRAL COLUMN IN STUDIES FROM NATURE

The way in which mounds and hollows succeed one another in the line of the back underlines both functional and psychological factors and the position of the body in space. It is therefore advisable first of all to grasp the disposition of the vertebral column as a vehicle of expression.

Bottom right: the clarification process is complete, and drawing has been reduced to a minimum, highlighting dynamics and the gradients of the shapes.

Drawing pen and Indian ink on A3-size paper

Section 7.1
Studies of the vertebral column as a structure creating form

103a MORE FINISHED STUDY FROM NATURE

The drama of feeding-time is over and peace again reigns, providing an opportunity to elaborate the study in terms of solidity, intersections and detail. The graphic artist must use this elaborating phase to bring together and assimilate a larger range of impressions.
Red chalk on A3-size paper

103b   Opaque paint on A4-size paper

Here we only touch on the impact of the mechanics of the vertebral column on changes of shape in the thorax. Let us at least look at the latter's behavior when the vertebral column is twisted laterally (fig. 104). The framework of the thorax and the shape of the ribs has to be compressed on the side of the concave curve, and stretched on the opposite side where the convexity of the side of thorax is further emphasized.

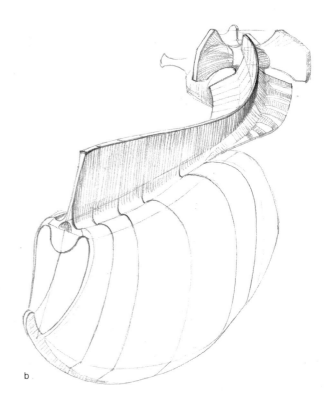

b

104a BEHAVIOR OF THE THORAX WHEN THE VERTEBRAL COLUMN BENDS LATERALLY

If the convex stresses of the thorax are visualized, it is easy to reconstruct its formal behavior. Accordingly the convexity on the inwardly curving side of the thorax is compressed, while the opposite side is extended.

104b VISUALIZATION OF A LATERAL BEND IN THE VERTEBRAL COLUMN OF A DOG

The backbone shape created by the spinous processes is shown as a laterally curved, upstanding strip, while the transverse processes on the convex side are more widely spaced and those on the concave side move closer together.

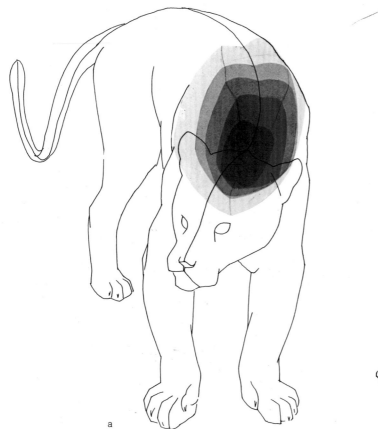

a

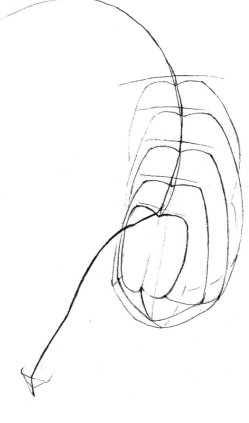

Section 7.1

Studies of the vertebral column as a structure creating form

105 STEPS TOWARD
UNDERSTANDING TORSION OF
THE VERTEBRAL COLUMN

a) Drawing based on a piece of Plasticine
modeled to represent the twisted trunk.
b, c) The same in front view with
powerful foreshortening.

d) Plasticine model, side view.
e) Using what has been learnt from (d) to
approximate the visualized organic form.
f) Study from imagination using
perceptions gained from the Plasticine
model.

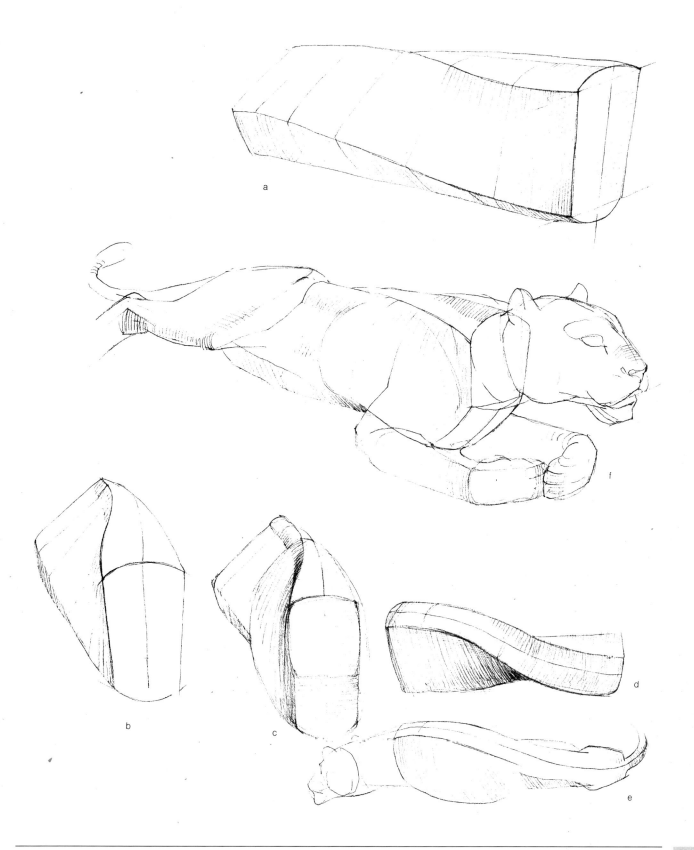

7.2

Drawing the thorax as a plastic core

The complex of the thorax takes the shape of a vessel with typical curves and dimensions. Let us look at its basic constructional features (fig. 106):

- overall convexity in the direction of stress from the back to the stomach and from front to back;
- the decreasing size of the anterior thoracic opening which is the main basis for the cross-section shape of the neck;
- the increasing size of the posterior thoracic opening, though its width may vary (passage to the herbivores' large intestinal tract or the carnivores' narrow one);
- the flexible, movable gridwork of the ribs and their costal cartilages (with wide variation in the number of ribs);
- the thorax connected by articular attachments to the vertebral column at the back, and on the abdominal side finishing at the sternum to which most ribs (the 'true' ribs) are joined.

Differences in the thorax as between one animal type and another are reflected in its dimensions (fig. 106):

- *Human being*: the shape is compressed between the chest and vertebral column, with a marked reduction in the size of the thorax to give balance in upright stance, but is considerably wider from side to side. In cross-section it is kidney-shaped.
- *Dog*: the sides are compressed with great depth between the stomach and vertebral column typical of a runner. In cross-section it is like a blunt-tipped almond standing on end.
- *Lion*: in cross-section it is almost the reverse of the dog's, an almond shape with the narrower end pointing up to the back, the blunt end down to the stomach.
- *Horse*: asymmetrical barrel shape, with the flatter side uppermost.
- *Cow*: virtually symmetrical. Cross-section a blunt spindle shape.
- *Anthropoid ape*: almost as wide as it is deep (semi-upright stance). Cross-section virtually square, with rounded corners.

In fig. 106 the thorax is conceived as a plastic core, and is blocked in: this approximates to its appearance in graphic terms. The following criteria must be borne in mind when drawing it:

- To establish its layout: draw a line on both the back and the stomach logically following the course of the central line (line of symmetry), based on the relevant viewing angle.
- Draw in cross-sections of the thorax which change as we progress from front to back; those between the shoulders and forelegs are always narrower, those at the back become wider.
- In doing so, do not allow yourself to be diverted by the line of the ribs. Imagine the cross-sections intersecting the level of symmetry internally at right angles (fig. 109).
- The thorax should be drawn either as a closed block or as a hollow body.

- Apexes of curves should always be emphasized, as should the convergence of different spatial planes and gradients which appear as facets.
- Remember always to draw constructionally; indeterminate hatching can be a trap (fig. 109).

Anyone who has no access to animal skeletons should make models of differently shaped thoraxes and try drawing them. Here we depict them (three-dimensionally) in front view, cross-section and at various angles (fig. 108). It is also possible to take the outline of the profile view (fig. 101) as a guide. What can be learned from an actual model of a thorax?

- The body must be viewed from every conceivable angle (ensuring that there are no gaps in your ability to imagine it three-dimensionally).
- The technical practice gained in this preparatory stage will heighten your capacity to observe three-dimensionally and your sense of touch.
- And encourage a considerably deeper and more lasting inner comprehension of the form.

This study will ensure that when you look at the living animal, however much its thorax may be covered with hair, you are always aware of it as a plastic core.

106 SCULPTURAL SHAPE OF THE THORAXES OF VARIOUS ANIMALS, IN SIMPLIFIED BLOCK FORM
Depicting the thorax as an enclosed shape reinforces understanding of its importance as a plastic core. In all forms of the thorax — except in primates — note the narrow sides in the area of the shoulder girdle; also the considerably smaller thoracic mass of carnivores as opposed to herbivores.

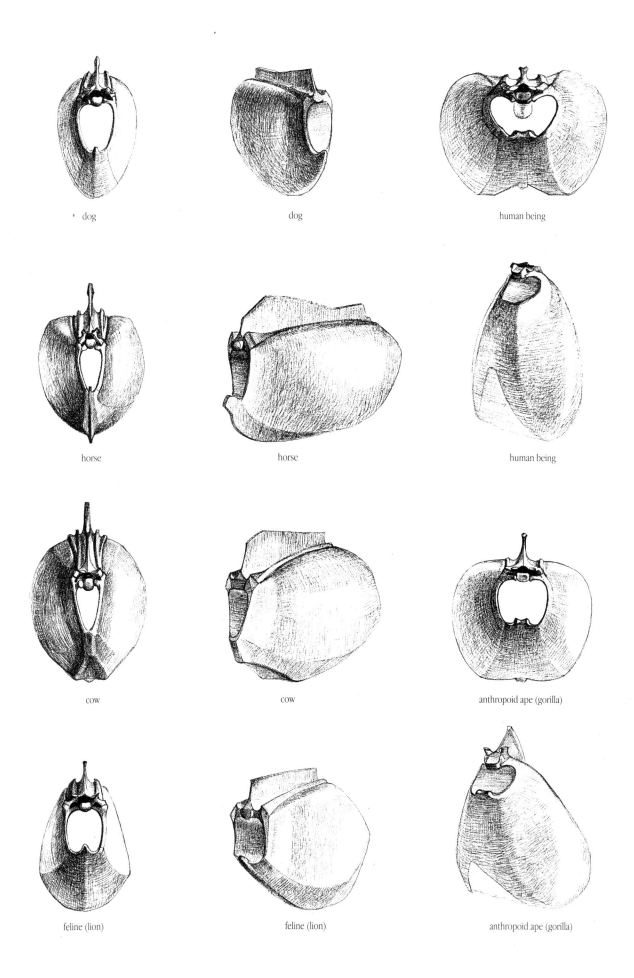

dog

dog

human being

horse

horse

human being

cow

cow

anthropoid ape (gorilla)

feline (lion)

feline (lion)

anthropoid ape (gorilla)

107 SIMPLIFIED THREE-QUARTER
FRONT VIEW OF A COW'S
THORAX

What is striking is the barrel-like expanse
of the herbivore's thorax at the end near
the pelvis, and its compressed shape
between the shoulder girdle.

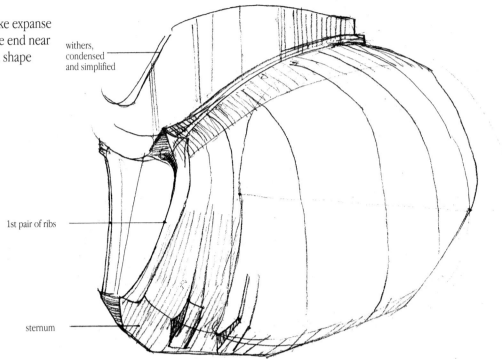

withers,
condensed
and simplified

1st pair of ribs

sternum

108 GRAPHIC SIMPLIFICATION OF A HORSE'S THORAX

The first impression is one of closed forms with varying degrees of
curvature. Lines drawn within the forms do not represent the ribs.
Model studies done by the author while teaching.

Pencil on A4-size paper

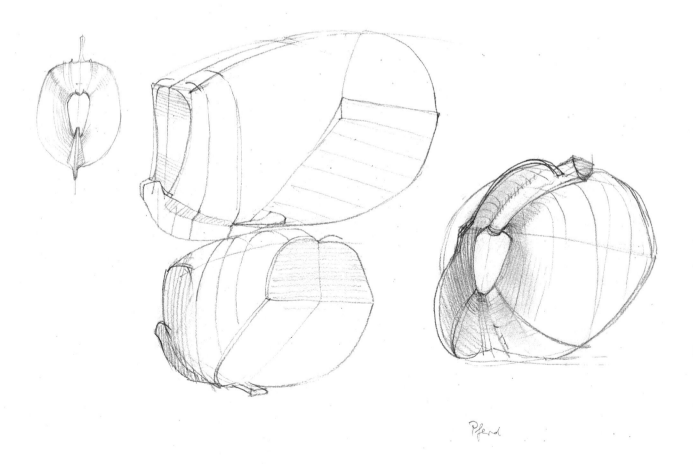

Section 7.2
Drawing the thorax as a plastic core

7.3
Drawing the skeleton of the whole trunk

Drawing the skeleton is always associated with the task of creating order. This means that:

- Everything must be in its right and proper place.
- The constructional design must show through as the predominant principle.
- The forms must be worked out as relating to their function.
- Construction and function must be clearly perceptible as constant and permanent elements.

Thus drawing the skeleton (fig. 109) involves:

- working like an architect, clarifying supporting and supported elements in their positions in space;
- determining the optical weight with which each component is perceived;
- awareness of comparative impressional qualities;
- determining the relative value of detail;
- understanding the configuration of forces, forms and directions with reference to the structural design and direct expression (gesture);
- simplifying forms so that functions and their interaction with other links in the working chain are clearly brought out.

These principles cannot be considered and realized independently of one another. The omission of any one of them from the drawing process would cause discrepancies in overall organization and order. What appears as structure includes contrasts of form and contrasts of substance. Drawing the complete skeleton of the trunk is again a preparatory stage for understanding the disposition and extent of the trunk muscles.

109 CONSTRUCTIONALLY SIMPLIFIED FORMS OF THE SKELETON OF A HERBIVORE (COW)
The simplifications relate primarily to the spinal column and the associated thorax which determine the shape of the line of the back and the body volume.
Vertical lines drawn on the thorax indicate where cross-sections of the different convex stresses would run.
Pencil on A3-size paper

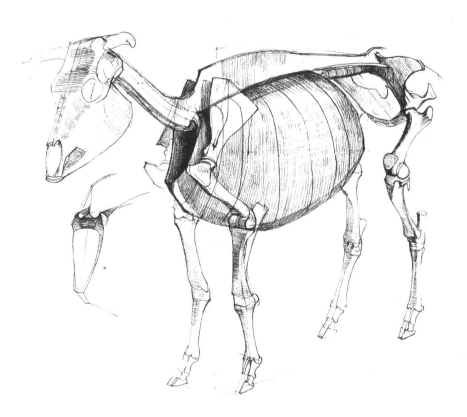

7.4

Disposition of the pure trunk muscles

As with the limbs, the disposition of the musculature is based on the three axes of the spinal column: through, transverse and longitudinal axes. The muscles extending inside the skeleton of the trunk are thin but wide, and therefore play an important role in forming the shape between the pelvis and vertebral column. Of the three differentiated functional groups of muscles, we need concentrate only on the pure trunk muscles (which close the gaps within the skeleton of the trunk).

It is worth nothing (fig. 111):

- the use of the pelvis and sacrum as the center of movement (where the muscles originate);
- insertion on the various levers on the spinal column (processes) and thorax (ribs).

These levers serve to:

- alter the sizes of the thorax and the abdominal cavity;
- alter the position of the thorax and spinal column relative to the pelvis;
- participate in respiration (back extensors assist breathing in), excretion and birth (pressing on abdomen);
- contribute to locomotive movement by extending and flexing the vertebral column.

Position and function:

- Muscles placed to the side of through-axes (running from back to stomach) of the spinal column effect lateral bending.
- Muscles lying above the transverse axes are extensors, those on the abdominal side are flexors.
- Muscles that cross the longitudinal axes diagonally are twisting muscles (for torsion).

Joint trunk-shoulder-girdle muscles and trunk-limb muscles are not dealt with here. Instead we must familiarize ourselves with the three most important trunk muscles, which shape the abdominal cavity on all sides, forming a cylinder:

- The *rectus abdominis* muscles originate at the pubic crest and tuberosities and are inserted into the sternum and the costal cartilage of the true ribs. They thus lie on the abdominal side of the transverse axes and make flexion of the vertebral column (convex arching) possible.
- The *spinal extensor muscles (common muscular mass)*, the counterpart of rectus abdominis, originate at the sacrum, pelvis and vertebral column and are inserted along the vertebral column to the front on the right and left of the spinous processes, particularly to the lumbar vertebrae: they form a powerful cord. They effect bending of the vertebral column (hollow arch, i.e. extension).
- *External oblique abdominal muscles* originate over a large area (ilium, pubic bone in the pelvis, lateral edge of rectus abdominis), and are inserted at the ribs. The fact that they cross the longitudinal axes of the vertebral column diagonally means that they effect torsion. They work with the rectus abdominis muscles (flexion of the vertebral column, lateral bending).

110 POSITIONS OF THE PURE TRUNK MUSCLES IN RELATION TO THE AXES OF THE VERTEBRAL COLUMN (CROSS-SECTION IN FRONT OF THE PELVIS)

The vertical through-axes (running from back to stomach) make it possible for the trunk to bend laterally, the horizontal longitudinal axis through the bodies of the vertebrae makes it possible for that axis to twist (torsion), and the transverse axes allow flexion and extension. The positions of the muscles relative to the various axes indicate.

111 DISPOSITION AND FORM OF PURE TRUNK AND NECK MUSCLES

a) Spinal extensor muscles, rectus abdominis, transversus abdominis, pectoral wall muscles and some neck muscles of the dog.

b) Similar illustration of the muscles of the horse, but including the external oblique muscles and more neck muscles.

a

b

c

d

- Ultimately the guiding framework can disappear entirely from the drawing (d).
  Drawing in an animal's coat, e.g. a tiger's stripes, can be a welcome device for underlining the solidity of the figure still further, as the stripes run round the body like cross-sections (fig. 116).
- It is important to put feeling into your picture, emphasizing some areas, understating others and creating curving, floating transitions into space (fig. 116).
- Create an optical center which attracts the gaze of the observer, perhaps part of the body or the head and the eyes (fig. 116).

The head and the expression produced by it are undoubtedly peculiarly important when human beings and animals face one another.

117 STARTING TO COMBINE KNOWLEDGE OF FORM WITH USE OF COLOR

There is no great shift in moving from a graphic study to one involving color, particularly as the contour effect of the black is very close to a drawn line of the back.

Panther walking. Watercolor and pen on a ground colored with acrylic, worked over with oil pastel and pure turpentine, A4-size paper

Section 7.5
Graphic aids to depicting the body

8.

Head forms

The living head is the combination of a number of formal components of various constitution: the bony skull and its soft forms such as muscle, skin, cartilage, connective tissue and sensory organs. The construction of the skull must again be regarded as the most important thing, and as with the limbs, we shall examine how the various formal features fit together. It is the interaction of the functional and constructional formal features that gives the image of *skull types*. Only then need we familiarize ourselves with the other formal components relating to soft forms.

One of the essential formal features of animal structural design is that the head with its sensory organs and feeding equipment should be at the front, as one pole of the horizontal organization of the body. The disposition of the totally concealed site of the brain, the protected sensory organs, the feeding apparatus is what gives distinctive form to the head and skull. The character of each animal type is most cogently concentrated here, its rank in the hierarchy; it is on the head that we find such distinctive features as manes, whiskers, colored markings, horns and antlers – show qualities.

This brings a new factor into our consideration of constructional components of form: self-advertisement. There are forehead attires and hair claddings as well as weird and wonderful colorings which defy analysis in terms of pure practicality.

Just as we have learned that the shape and course of the line of the back or the limbs can typify a species, so the head with its individual gestures and attitude can be understood as a direct expression of inner mood. On the other hand, in looking at the line of the back with the head at the front we also discovered species – specific ways of carrying the head that have nothing whatsoever to do with any particular, transitory state of mind, but are permanent postures with no psychological implications.

In the following sections we shall look closely at the construction of the skull in our chosen animal types.

8.1
Types of skull structures

The skull consists of two sections, the *cranial skull* and the *facial skull* (including the lower jaw or mandible). The former is a protective, closed, ovoid capsule for the brain, and whereas in human beings it is the upper part of the skull, in animals it is the rear part.

The facial skull in all its subtle diversity, with hollows, grooves, openings, breaks, curves, ledges and sharp edges, is directed forward and precedes the cranial skull in space. This produces the predominating horizontal direction from the tip of the muzzle to the ledge marking the back of the head. The general structural design of an animal is dependent on this crucial direction. The following factors relating to the form and mass of the two sections have general application (figs 118, 119):

● the degree of the development of the brain and its mass;
● the function and importance of the sensitive sensory organs (eyes, nose, ears);
● the performance and construction of the tools relating to ingesting and breaking up food (chewing equipment).

The *cranial skull* is enclosed by areas that can be designated:
● the forehead;
● the crown of the head;
● the temples;
● the back of the head;
● the base of the skull (concealed).

The division between the cranial and facial skull varies according to the type of skull and cannot always be depicted in the same way. The course of the base of the skull (a thin-boned bottom lid to the skull capsule) can more or less be followed using these guidelines:

● in *apes* it runs from the jutting brow (ledge above the eyes);
● in *carnivores* from a bend in the line of the profile;
● in *horses* from just above the widest point of the skull;
● and in *cows* a little higher above the widest point of the skull.

The base of the skull then runs down from this front demarcation to the opening of the auditory canal. After that it cannot be followed because it is covered by neck muscles. At the sides (on the temples), the skull capsule is enclosed by masticatory muscles, to the rear by the back of the neck and head (where the cervical muscles are inserted), and on top by the small, flat forehead.

Skull construction reveals species – specific structural forms relating to adaptation to ways of life, differing as between the herbivore (fig. 123), the carnivore (fig. 119), and the ape (fig. 118).

There are variations between different species of herbivore, but the size of the facial skull with the long nasal passage, powerful grinding and crushing teeth, lateral position of the eyes with a bony annular eye frame and a small cranial skull are common to all herbivores. The overall form is like a trihedral prism.

Form of the horse's skull (fig. 120)

- The horse's facial skull has a long pyramidal shape that is compressed laterally.
- There is a huge ridge of bone near the nape of the neck marking the rear end of the skull capsule (insertion of the flexible nuchal ligament).
- There is a weak ridge of bone at the top of the skull capsule that stops and forks in the forehead area, forming part of the orbital ring with a bridge to the zygomatic arch.
- The nasal passage narrows as it approaches the muzzle and comes out at the tip of the twin nasal bones.
- The back of the nose is straight and slim, widening at the sides to the upper jaw. Here there is a sharp-edged stepped angle, forming a crest in the cheek which is a typical feature of the horse.
- There are rows of incisor teeth in the upper and lower jaws, which close at the front like biting tongs.
- There is a gap between the molar and incisor teeth.
- The powerful, almost rectangular lower jaw has a rising branch going up to the pivotal point (temporo-maxillary joint). The branch forks into a condyloid process carrying the joint roller and a coronoid process (where the masticatory muscle is inserted).
- The transition from the cheek crest to the zygomatic arch is shaped like a handle.

Form of the cow's skull

- The skull is short, massive, squat and broad.
- The basic shape is pyramidal as in the horse, but less compressed laterally (approximately a trihedral prism).
- The end of the cranial skull is indicated on the back of the neck by an obtuse, transversely rectangular area where muscles are inserted.

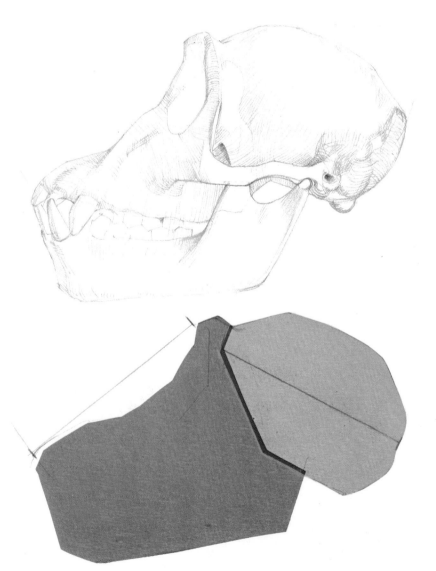

118 SKULL OF AN ANTHROPOID APE (CHIMPANZEE), EMPHASIZING THE SECTIONS OF THE SKULL

In the anthropoid ape the size of the facial skull (brown) is greater than that of the cranial skull (khaki), which falls from the brow ridge toward the nape of the neck.

119 SKULL OF A CARNIVORE (LION), EMPHASIZING THE LINE OF THE PROFILE AND SHOWING THE RELATIONSHIP BETWEEN THE CRANIAL AND FACIAL SKULL

Lines of equal length each corresponding to a measurement of the cranial skull are marked in red. The characteristic bend in the profile of the feline skull forms an angle of about 150°.

In the extremely simplified lower drawing the size of the cranial skull (dark shading) in relation to the rest of the skull is indicated.

Section 8.1
Types of skull structures

- There is a swollen thickening between the horns (crest of the frontal bone) marking the highest and farthest back curve of the cranial skull.
- The area between the orbital cavities and this crest has a regular rectangular shape.
- The nasal area is blunt.
- The cheek crest is not pronounced.
- There are no incisors in the upper jawbone.
- The short, strong zygomatic arch runs from the orbital cavity to the opening of the auditory canal.
- The forehead-nose profile is almost perfectly straight.
- The lower jaw from the incisor teeth to the angle of the jaw forms a convex curve.

Skull of the carnivore

The relationship between the size of the cranial and facial skulls shifts little in favor of the cranial skull. The facial skull is shorter and less bulky. The overall appearance suggests an almost ovoid shape with the jawbones jutting out as an independent form. The shape of the teeth, including the dagger-shaped canines and jagged side teeth equipped with a polished cutting edge, is adapted to breaking bones and cutting through meat. Other features common to all carnivores are:

- a bend in the line of the profile where the facial skull meets the cranial skull (especially pronounced in felines);
- reduced size of the masticatory apparatus (crushing and cutting). The food is not chewed after being cut up, but swallowed (swallowing skull);
- very large coronoid process on the branch of the jawbone;
- zygomatic arch forming a powerful handle shape jutting out sharply to the side;
- protective hollow for the eyeball is only a groove (ocular groove);

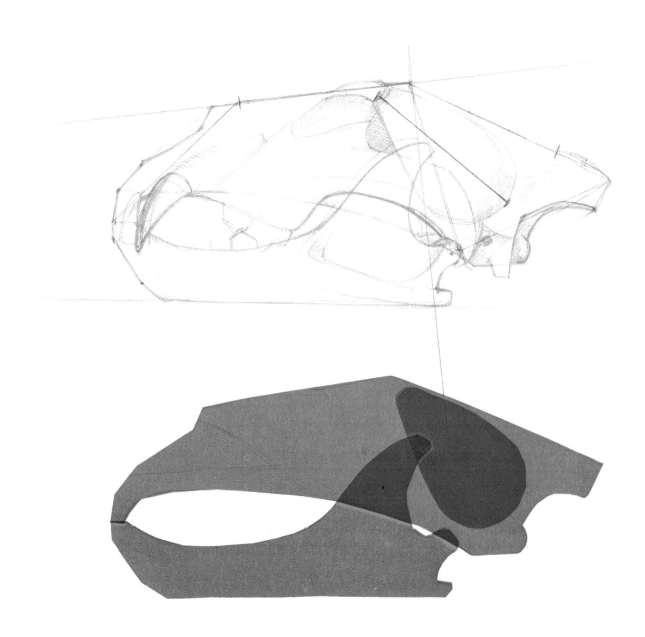

- eyes positioned to look forward (accurate three-dimensional vision for seizing prey);
- powerful bony ridge on the crown of the head and at the end of the cranial skull (point of origin of the masticatory muscles, insertion of cervical muscles).

Shape of the dog's skull (figs 122, 125)
- The basic form is ovoid with the blunt end at the back of the head.
- The tip of the muzzle and the nape of the neck are on exactly the same horizontal level.

- The surface of the neck is triangular with a sharp point (crest-like protuberance on the posterior occipital bone).
- There is a crest on the crown of the cranial skull like the ridge on a helmet.
- The parietal crest forks and arches down to the ocular groove, forming a hook-like process of the frontal bone, matched below by a hook-like process of the jawbone.
- The condyle of the lower jaw sits in a cavity of the very projecting zygomatic arch and under the lateral curve of the skull capsule (transmission of masticatory pressure).

120 DIFFERENT TYPES OF SKULL DRAWN CONSTRUCTIONALLY

a) Three-quarter rear view of a horse's skull tipped slightly to one side.
b) View into the open skull capsule from behind, with the occipital bone removed.
c) Leopard's skull with open jaw.

d) Skull of a female gorilla.
Observe how the way in which the forms continue and cross one another on both sides has been made visible.

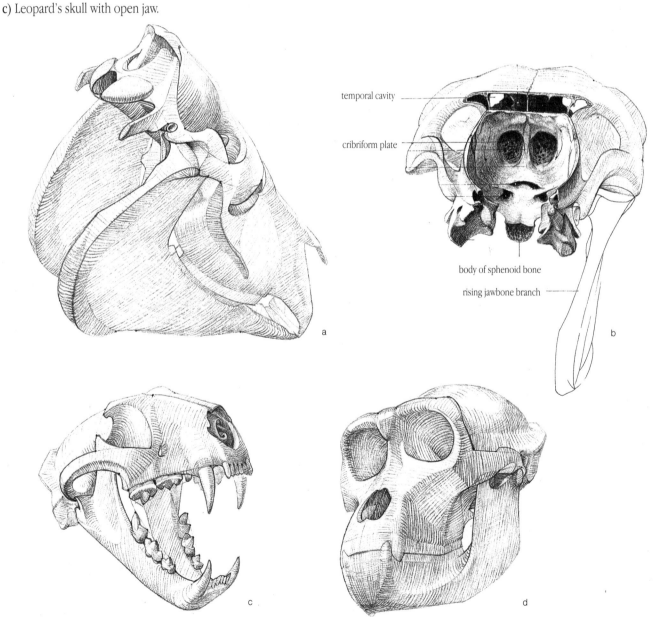

temporal cavity

cribriform plate

body of sphenoid bone

rising jawbone branch

a

b

c

d

Section 8.1
Types of skull structures

- The zygomatic arch joins the area at the back of the teeth and cheeks (here too masticatory pressure is transmitted onto the jawbone).
- The profile line of the lower jaw near the cheek and teeth forms a very shallow curve.

Altogether the shape of the dog's skull is reminiscent of Gothic architecture. Like the rest of its build, the skull is graceful (a hunter that pursues its prey).

Shape of the lion's skull (figs 119, 124)

Most of the differences in the cranial skull between the lion and other animal types relate to proportion:

- The shape is a compressed, blunt ovoid (note the shortness of the facial skull), with the greatest width being a little more than half the length of the skull.
- A large shelving bend in the profile line at the transition from the facial to the cranial skull (especially in the tiger, panther and domestic cat).
- The zygomatic arches jut out to the side to an exceptional degree (as in the dog they form the widest head measurement).
- The ocular groove is directed straight forward.
- The line of symmetry on the skull near the nasal and temporal bone is marked by a clear groove.

Altogether the lion's skull is reminiscent of Baroque architecture. It is heavy and massive, corresponding to the generally athletic build of a hunter that lies in wait for its prey.

Skull of the anthropoid ape (figs 118, 120d)

- The cranial skull no longer seems like an appendage inside a considerably larger overall form consisting of the facial skull. Its size and visibility make it recognizable in its own right, and it has a considerable impact on the shape of the head and skull.
- The two parts of the skull are clearly separated by a ridge above the eyes (brow protuberance), and in profile there is a sharp bend between the facial and the cranial skull.
- The eyes are sunk in hollow pyramids enclosed on all sides, the bases of which lie close together and nearly vertically, forming the apexes of the pyramids deep under the base of the skull.
- The position of the orbital cavity is directed straight to the front (controlling the activity of the hands).
- The nasal passage is quite shallow, short and sunken so that even the soft nose projects very little in profile, or not at all.
- The upper and lower jaw project relatively far out, continued by the position of the incisor teeth.
- The incisor teeth areas of the upper and lower jaw meet in an obtuse to right angle, and the chin has no point.
- The canines are distinct cones standing out from the other teeth, and the molars have broad, masticating crowns.
- The rising branch of the jawbone ranges from slender to powerful (especially in the gorilla).
- The zygomatic arch is relatively slender and in comparison with carnivores the curve is slight.

- The cranial skull of males may have great bony ridges (the gorilla) or not (the chimpanzee).

The central column of the face – a continuous connection running from the front of the lower jawbone, via the upper jaw, the passage of the nose and the inner wall of the orbital cavity – transmits masticatory pressure to below the base of the skull where it is diverted to its horizontal surface. From the rising branch of the jawbone upward the masticatory pressure is taken over by the temporal area and cancelled in the crown of the head.

The construction of the types of skull described is thus determined by the spaces enclosed (cranial capsule, nasal and oral cavities) and by the reinforcing directions accepting the masticatory pressure which run from the front of the lower jaw to the crown of the head. The way in which main forms stand out, their formal connections, the subordinate character of the secondary, transitional and bridging forms are all linked with this way of looking at things. This is an ordered framework which exists objectively, and has been made transparently clear: it attains its highest form of architectonic development in the skull. This framework character is also the theme of constructional drawing of the skull.

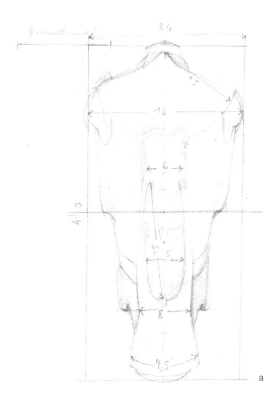

a

121 PROPORTIONAL STUDY OF THE SKULL OF A HERBIVORE (HORSE)

Frontal view of skull indicating the relationship between height and width. Measurements in centimeters

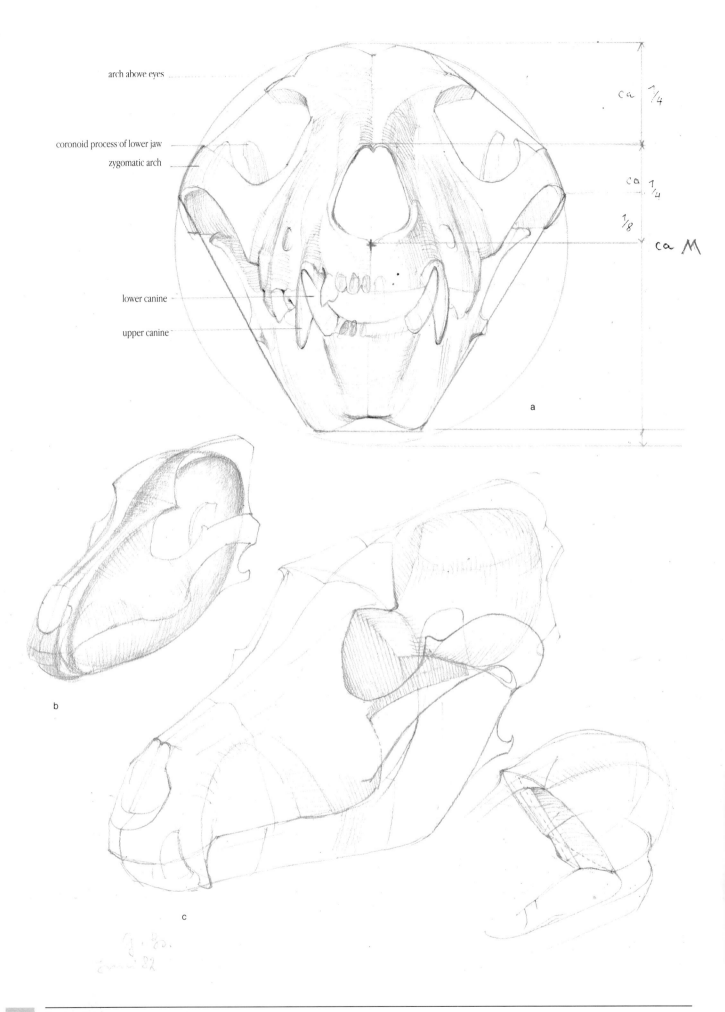

arch above eyes

coronoid process of lower jaw

zygomatic arch

lower canine

upper canine

ca $\frac{1}{4}$

ca $\frac{1}{4}$

$\frac{1}{8}$

ca M

a

b

c

Section 8.1
Types of skull structures

8.2
Drawing the skull constructionally

The constructionally determined forms of the skull undergo further adaptation to meet the demands of graphic design. Concealed forms, directions, corners and sharp edges drawn to show (fig. 123):

- The skull shape with its many components is simplified and reduced to the block-like shape which essentially expresses the skull type (a).
- After this rough shape of the greater whole has been established, graduated surface planes can be drawn in (b).
- The skull should be treated as a crystalline structure with polished facets and curves, which can be emphasized by drawing in cross-sections where you think they should be (b).
- These help in the basic organization of the areas of hatching conveying modeling – this has nothing to do with shading.
- In line with our previous graphic approach, the skull too should be laid out according to a spatial reference system on the line of symmetry and the three-dimensional cross-axes intersecting it, (a).
- This should all be followed through logically in drawing (a).

122 PROPORTIONS OF A DOG'S SKULL VIEWED FRONTALLY AND THREE-DIMENSIONALLY

a) The greatest width and height of the skull can virtually be inscribed in a circle with its center at the start of the nose. If the points of the skull are joined this produces a pentagon (red lines).
b) The ovoid shape of the skull is emphasized, with only a few subsidiary shapes projecting beyond the 'egg'.
c) Cranial and facial skull viewed three-dimensionally showing the spatial planes and gradients with the help of cross sections.

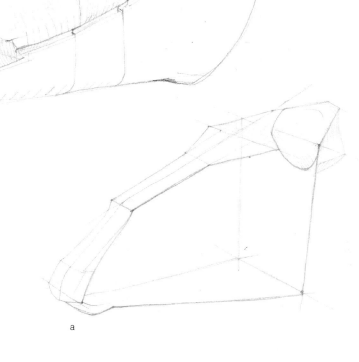

b

123 SIMPLIFYING FORMS AS A PRELIMINARY TO CONVEYING THE ACTUAL SHAPE WITH ITS MANY COMPONENTS (HORSE)

a) Simplification based on a trihedral prism allowing the basic three-dimensional factors to be checked easily.
b) Constructionally simplified actual shape of the skull, with the spatial directions indicated by lines following the cross-sections.

a

124 ARCHITECTURALLY INTERPRETED
SKULL SHAPE (LION)

The architectural nature of the lion's features only becomes striking when a large number of components is inserted into the shape – here in the 'Baroque style'.

a) Solid, three-dimensional view. Similar or identical directions in the gradients of the planes and how they continue are worked out as connections.

b, c) The same skull with an open jaw, revealing the hollows and dome-like vaulting as the essential formal images and highlighting their 'Baroque' appearance.

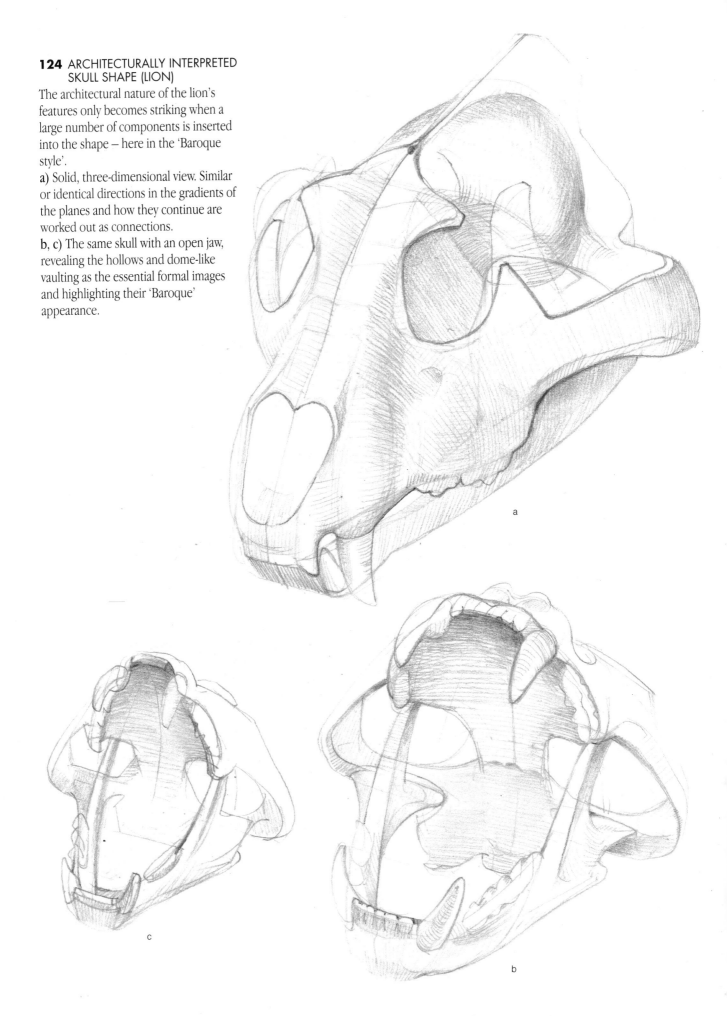

a

c

b

Section 8.2
Drawing the skull constructionally

- Set about your work like an architect, i.e. explore the groundplan shapes of the cranial and facial skull, erect the walls of the building, its domes, vaulted apexes, cantilevered arches etc. above the groundplan.
- It is best to choose planes and gradients that provide good three-dimensional contrasts (made easier by reducing the forms to elements as has already been done).

Drawing the skull constructionally is one of the most interesting and instructive tasks in drawing, though one of the most difficult. It trains the ability to imagine appearances like no other method of drawing, for the skull is in fact the determining formal basis of the head. Drawing the skull constructionally creates distillations of form and excludes mere acceptance of externals. The figures in section 8.1 all convey the constructional nature of different types of skull and how to set them out graphically in constructional terms. In case the student is unable to find life models, the figures also set out to impart a minimal ability to visualize the essentially different types of skull, serving as bridges between thinking what is inside and determining what is outside.

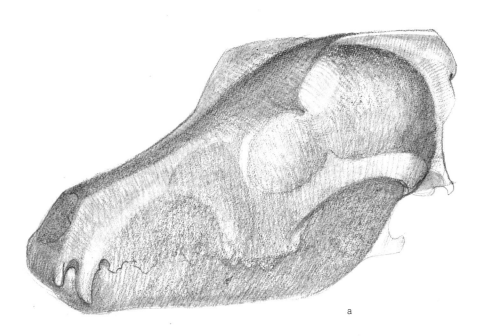

a

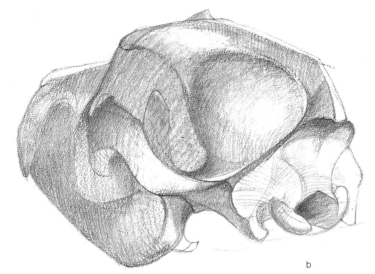

b

125 GRACEFUL ARCHITECTURE OF THE SKULL (DOG)
The slenderness and delicacy of a dog's skull is reminiscent of Gothic architecture. Both these studies attempt to give a complex condensation of the form of the skull with its many details as a pointed ovoid shape.
a) Three-quarter front view of skull, indicating its most important subsidiary forms.
b) The same skull, three-quarter back view, revealing the end of the skull with its bony ridges arranged like a frame.

8.3
The head and the shapes of its soft parts

The soft parts are all those parts of the head that are not bony. They can change shape to suit the activities of the eyes, nose, mouth and ears. They also include the muscles of the head (masticatory and facial muscles). The component forms include the eyes, nose, mouth and ears.

Muscles of the head (fig. 126)

These are very briefly considered by reviewing the directions they follow:

- Muscles concerned with chewing are the bulky masticatory muscles which move the temporo-maxillary joint and press the lower jaw against the upper jaw, originating at the jawbone or cheek crest (horse and cow) and being inserted at the angle and climbing branch of the jawbone (thick and bulky in carnivores).
- Facial muscles concerned with opening and shutting sensory organ apertures originate from a fixed base, the skull, but are inserted in the malleable cutaneous parts surrounding the apertures. Annular muscles close the apertures, while radially arranged ones open them.

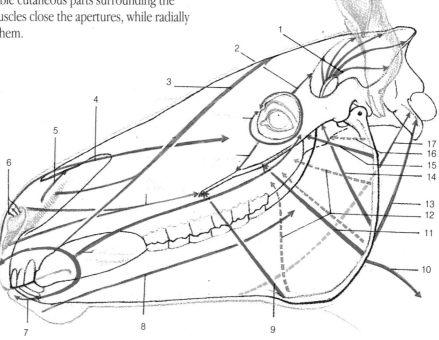

126a MUSCLE SYSTEM IN A HORSE'S HEAD

The system of muscles operating the opening and closing of the jaw and of sensory apertures is shown as a network of directional lines. Note the position of the masticatory muscles in relation to the pivotal point of the temporo-maxillary joint (red arrows indicate pulling direction of muscles effecting closing, blue arrows those effecting opening). Red circular muscles operate closure of the sensory organs, blue lines represent muscles that open the apertures.

1	temporal muscles
2	ocular muscles
3	levator of nose and lip
4	levator of upper lip
5	nasal muscle
6	transverse nasal muscle
7	annular mouth muscle
8	abductor of lower lip
9	masseter (masticatory muscle)
10	pectoro-maxillary muscle
11	masseter (masticatory muscle)
12	internal alar muscle
13	throat-jaw muscle
14	jawbone section of masseter
15	masseter
16	external alar muscle
17	biventral muscle of the lower jaw

Among the masticatory muscles that merit special mention are the masseter (figs 126, 127, 128, 129) and the temporal muscle, the former because of its impact on the shape of the cheek, the latter because it covers the area of the temple, having a considerable plastic effect in carnivores and anthropoid apes.

The facial muscles, however, none of which has to operate a bony lever as they virtually only have to move the skin, are not bulky and have very little plastic impact on appearance. Their effects on the skin in opening or closing the sensory apertures do nonetheless produce creases and wrinkles which also serve as spontaneous signs of mental and psychological states and are perceived as conveying intelligible messages in contact between animals or between animals and human beings: baring the teeth and laying the ears back as threatening gestures, rolling the eyes in terror, wrinkling the back of the nose as a result of raising the upper lip, flaring the nostrils.

126b PARTS AND MUSCLES OF THE HEAD VIEWED FROM ABOVE

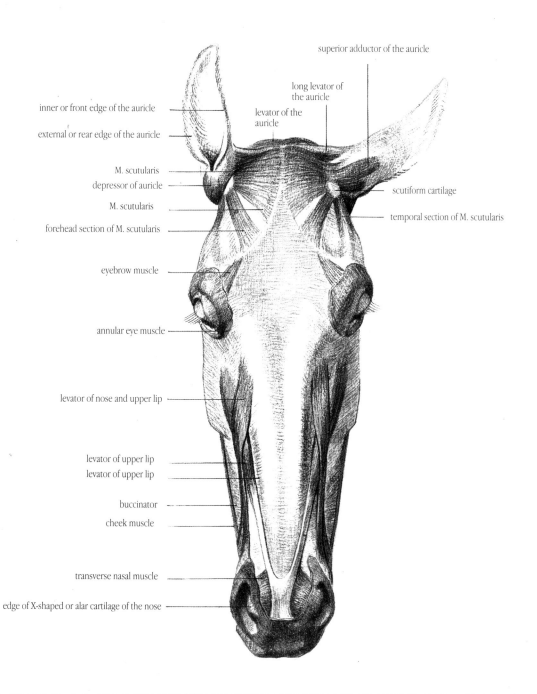

superior adductor of the auricle

long levator of the auricle

inner or front edge of the auricle

levator of the auricle

external or rear edge of the auricle

M. scutularis

depressor of auricle

scutiform cartilage

M. scutularis

temporal section of M. scutularis

forehead section of M. scutularis

eyebrow muscle

annular eye muscle

levator of nose and upper lip

levator of upper lip

levator of upper lip

buccinator

cheek muscle

transverse nasal muscle

edge of X-shaped or alar cartilage of the nose

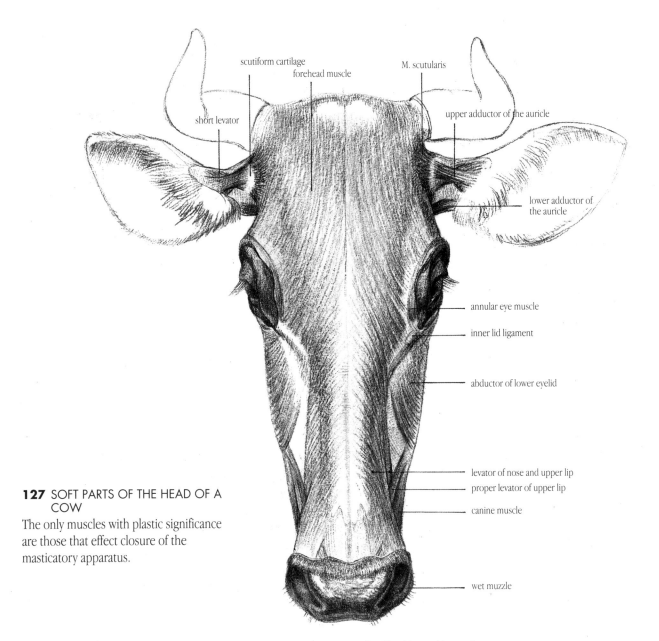

scutiform cartilage

forehead muscle

M. scutularis

short levator

upper adductor of the auricle

lower adductor of the auricle

annular eye muscle

inner lid ligament

abductor of lower eyelid

levator of nose and upper lip

proper levator of upper lip

canine muscle

wet muzzle

127 SOFT PARTS OF THE HEAD OF A COW

The only muscles with plastic significance are those that effect closure of the masticatory apparatus.

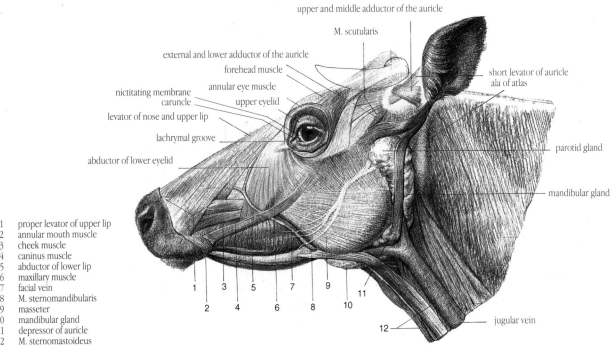

upper and middle adductor of the auricle

M. scutularis

external and lower adductor of the auricle

forehead muscle

short levator of auricle

ala of atlas

annular eye muscle

nictitating membrane

caruncle

upper eyelid

levator of nose and upper lip

lachrymal groove

parotid gland

abductor of lower eyelid

mandibular gland

1	proper levator of upper lip
2	annular mouth muscle
3	cheek muscle
4	caninus muscle
5	abductor of lower lip
6	maxillary muscle
7	facial vein
8	M. sternomandibularis
9	masseter
10	mandibular gland
11	depressor of auricle
12	M. sternomastoideus

1 3 5 7 9 11
 2 4 6 8 10

12

jugular vein

Section 8.3
The head and the shapes of its soft parts

Only muscles making up the masticatory
apparatus are significant in plastic terms:
the skull is rounded to an ovoid shape by
the temporal and masticatory muscles.

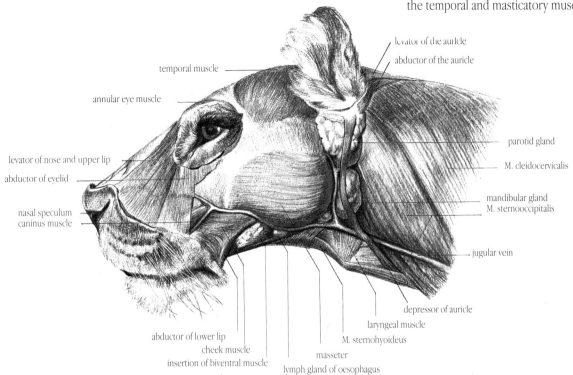

levator of the auricle
abductor of the auricle
temporal muscle
annular eye muscle
parotid gland
M. cleidocervicalis
levator of nose and upper lip
abductor of eyelid
mandibular gland
M. sternooccipitalis
nasal speculum
caninus muscle
jugular vein
depressor of auricle
laryngeal muscle
abductor of lower lip
cheek muscle
M. sternohyoideus
insertion of biventral muscle
masseter
lymph gland of oesophagus

129 SOFT PARTS OF THE HEAD OF A
DOG

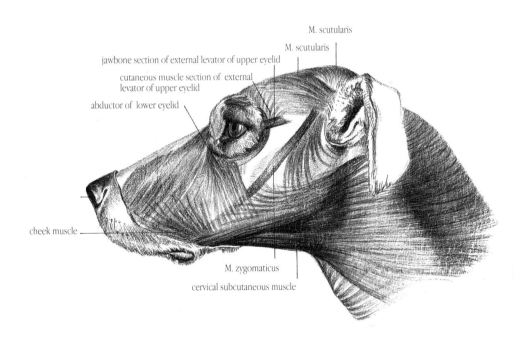

M. scutularis
M. scutularis
jawbone section of external levator of upper eyelid
cutaneous muscle section of external
levator of upper eyelid
abductor of lower eyelid
cheek muscle
M. zygomaticus
cervical subcutaneous muscle

130 PARTS OF THE HEAD OF A
CARNIVORE (DOG) ASSEMBLED

a) Combination of forms in the head as a whole.

b) Shapes and directions of the planes of the head.

c) The eye viewed in profile.

d) Frontal view of the eye.

e) Frontal view of the nasal speculum.

f) Protruding soft nose viewed in profile with side slits of the nostrils.

Section 8.3
The head and the shapes of its soft parts

Shapes and plasticity of the eye
The only factor common to all animals is that the spherical glassy body of the eyeball, surrounded by membrane, is opened and closed. The shape formed by the eyelids and the position of the eyeball within them vary from species to species. In drawing the eye of the horse – used as a representative example – the following principles should be followed (fig. 131):

- The eye is placed at the side of the head (typical of animals that take flight). Seen from the front the eye is foreshortened.
- The three-dimensional effects of the overlapping of the eyeball and eyelids must be conveyed.
- The upper lid must be distinguished from the covering fold located above it by the crease in the upper lid.

- It should never be forgotten that the area directly round the eye represents the plastic continuation of the shape of the eyeball. Its spherical form and the lids covering it are very similar to those of a horse chestnut bursting out of its skin.
- The lids themselves have mass, so that the eyeball is not in fact popped into a paper-thin mask-like cut-out sector.
- In herbivores the inner corner of the eye is a little more recessed than the outer corner, in carnivores much more so (figs 128, 129).
- There are no eyelashes on the lower lid.
- The iris is a browny-yellow color.
- The shape of the pupil (in ungulates and ruminants) is transversely oval, while in cats it is vertical.

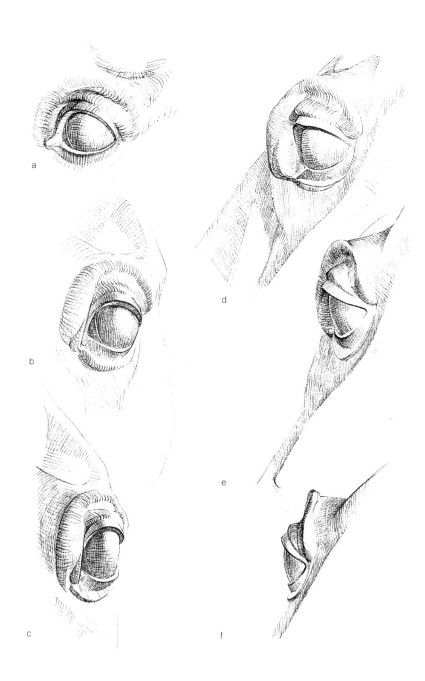

131 THINGS TO NOTE WHEN DRAWING THE EYE OF A HORSE
The drawing must make the eye intelligible as a sphere surrounded by the cover of the eyelids which follow its shape. Viewed from all angles eyeball and eyelids overlap and intersect, and this is important in depicting the eye.
a) Full view
b) Three-quarter front view
c) Front view
d) Side view
e) Three-quarter rear view
f) Rear view

Shapes and plasticity of the nose and mouth
The closeness of the nose and mouth to one another means they are often mutually dependent in function and form. The dog's nose (fig. 129), which protrudes a long way, is an organ for picking up scent on the ground, protruding even beyond the upper lip. The way in which the lips of many herbivores protrude beyond the nose is adapted to taking food, though the lips and nose of the cow (fig. 127) extend to about the same point. In carnivores (figs 128, 129) the corner of the mouth is elongated because of a loose flap of skin (chops), spare skin enabling the jaws to open wide.

Nose and mouth of the horse (fig. 126)
- On the right and left of the nasal septum cartilage there is bag-shaped elongated cartilage and connective tissue, forming the nostrils.
- These are not as far forward as the front section of the lips, and are nearer to the lip than in the cow.
- The shape of the nostril is like a tilted C, with the break occurring near the top, a little to the side.
- The upper lip starts directly below the nostrils.
- The corner of the mouth is surrounded by seams.
- The upper and lower lip are supported from behind by upper and lower incisors.
- The part of the lower lip in front of the incisors has a swollen roundness, at the back it develops into a dome-shaped mound of connective tissue. There is a velvety covering of hair on both upper and lower lip.

Nose and mouth of the cow (fig. 132)
- The nose and mouth are wide and blunt.
- The nostrils are farther apart than in the horse and more compact.
- The shape of the nostrils resembles an upturning spiral, with the blunt end near the lips.
- The nostrils are directed more to the sides than the front.
- The area between the nostrils and the mouth fissure is damp and therefore gleaming.
- The sides of the upper lip overhang the corner of the mouth.
- The nose and mouth are suspended at an obtuse angle above the bony brace of the upper jaw (which has no incisor teeth).
- From the front edge of the lower lip extending out and to the side there is a baggy thickening of the connective tissue.

Nose and mouth of the dog (fig. 129)
According to the breed of dog there are variations from the bluntest shape (bulldog) to the most elongated (greyhound).
- The soft nose is made up of tube-shaped cartilage.
- The wings of the nose and the speculum in front view vary from a rounded-off lozenge shape to a circle; in profile they are triangular.
- The speculum has a shallow, vertical notch between the nostrils which carries on down to the upper lip and the mouth.
- The sides of the nose fold up in a curve and are damp and gleaming. The nostril forms a slit in profile.

- The side of the upper lip swells in a curve (pushed out by the two canines in the upper and lower jaw).
- The mouth fissure rises in a shallow angle, running up into the chops at the side and the corner of the mouth.
- The edges of the lips have virtually no mass of their own.
- On the front and side of the upper lip there are several overlapping rows of tactile hairs.

Nose and mouth of the big cat (fig. 128)
- The profile from the nose to the lower jaw almost ends in a right angle (because of the projecting nasal speculum), the upper lip has tactile hairs, and there is hair on the chin.
- The nasal speculum forms a low, wide Y-shape.
- The central axis of the speculum is marked by a shallow, vertical groove continuing into the upper lip and down to the mouth fissure.
- The wings of the nose flare back, and are rolled in.
- There are slit-like recesses round the sides of the wings of the nose.
- A small strip of the lips is hairless and dark-colored, the mouth fissure runs down from the center to the sides, and there are chops over the corners of the mouth.
- The sides of the upper lip are pushed out and supported by canines.
- There are several rows of tactile hairs in the upper lip.
- The lower lip has a fairly long, dense covering of hair.

Shapes and plasticity of the ear (figs 126, 127, 128, 129)
The outer ear consists of very flexible, malleable ear cartilage shaped like a bag with a pointed (herbivores), blunt-pointed (canines and domestic cats), or rounded (big cats and bears) opening. Near the skull the ear muscle travels through a stabilizing pipe which varies in length.

Shape of the horse's ear (fig. 126)
- The ear stands straight up.
- The inner and outer edge of the ear converge at the tip.
- The inner edge of the ear running up to the tip of the ear from the auricle opening is twisted.

Shape of the cow's ear (fig. 127)
- The ear is positioned at the side, protruding horizontally below the horn.
- The overall shape is like a spoon, but ending in a blunt tip.
- The auricle aperture is directed very much downward.
- The inner (or upper) edge of the ear running up to the tip of the ear from the auricle aperture is twisted.
- The outer (or lower) edge of the ear curves steeply down from the auricle aperture, then bends back toward the tip of the ear.
- The inner edge of the ear is far more hairy than the outer edge.

132 MODELING OF NOSE AND MOUTH OF THE COW
The blunt shape of the nose-mouth area results from the wide spacing of the nostrils, with the moist speculum between them and the corner of the mouth framed by the upper lip.

- In large cats, especially lions, the ear is a bluntly rounded shell-shape with no tip (in domestic cats there is a rounded tip).
- The auricle is positioned slightly on the slant and turned outward.
- The outer edge of the ear near the auricle aperture is often split, with a vertical pocket of skin. There is then a clear curve and the edge of the ear turns up.
- The inner (or front) edge of the ear is well covered with long tufts of hair.

Thus the component parts of the animals' heads vary with function and form: they do not constitute a constant, unchanging order.

8.4
Drawing the head as a whole

In drawing an animal's head we have of course to assimilate both the basic and subsidiary forms of each animal type. At the same time we feel driven to express the sensations we experience in looking at an animal's head; we want to grasp and animate our object with that drive.

We shall consider some qualities derived from subjective experience in the drawings reproduced on the following pages, which demonstrate that object and subject can be integrated to produce artistic unity, and we see this as a final phase of graphic study. But so that practical knowledge is not too easily sacrificed

133 BASIC FORM OF THE HEAD OF A HERBIVORE (HORSE)
The basic shape is a narrow triangular prism produced by the long facial skull and general lateral flattening, highlighted further by the flat vertical plane extending through the masseter from the cheek crest to the lower jaw.

134 BASIC FORM OF THE HEAD OF A CARNIVORE (LEOPARD)
The distinctive plastic features are the ovoid basic shape rounded by the masseter, the relatively short facial skull, the forward-looking eyes and the bend in the profile where the forehead meets the bony nose.

to subjective expressivity, in drawing the head building with masses and structures must again come first (figs 133, 134).

The features of each skull type are not fundamentally weakened by the soft forms. On the contrary, these round and close gaps in the skeletal shapes, giving the living appearance its formal unity. This makes us aware of basic shapes such as the trihedral prism typical of herbivores or the ovoid of carnivores, irrespective of whether the masticatory muscles in the cheek, jawbone-angle area make the cheek into a flat, vertical facet of a trihedral prism (as in herbivores), a blunt ovoid shape (cats) or a long ovoid form (dogs). There are no muscles that stand out from the surface created by the skeleton.

In order to come to terms with textural and structural factors we again use hatching to follow the planes of the body in the following drawings.

Experiential qualities and a painter's ability to express them open up wide scope. In the early Renaissance a painterly concept of drawing was not yet widely accepted.

Pisanello (fig. 136a) for example conveys the plasticity of the horse's head, a well-modeled relief, using an extremely fine nib to depict the whorls of hair and the pile of the coat. He exploits the natural texture, to convey spatial contours and the tension of the curves.

This very analytical, classical Renaissance concept later lost ground to Impressionist ways of conveying appearance. Adolf Menzel (fig. 137) may serve as just one example among countless others. Much is conveyed by suggestion, painterly tonal values and blank areas. The liveliness of the expression lies in the controlled jotting, the glow of the coat, the way marks are woven together to produce textures that suggest color.

135 DISTINCTIVE FEATURES OF THE HEAD OF A BIG CAT IN FRONT VIEW (LIONESS)

Like the skull as a whole, the head in front view is shaped like a large pentagon, with the vertical central axis characterized by the furrow in the brow, the wide back of the nose, the relatively wide space between the eyes and the broad, shallow Y-shape of the speculum.

136a COAT TEXTURE AS AN ORGANIZING FACTOR IN DRAWING WITH A PEN

Before special painterly ways of seeing were developed in Baroque art, one of the most important tasks of art was to convey the form of natural objects with total clarity. The modeling of the relief of the head has been effected here by using extremely delicate hatching following the directions and texture of the coat: no attempt is made to convey color by graphic means.

Antonio Pisanello (1395-c. 1455), Horse's head in front view, with hanging harness.

Pen on white paper, 10¾ x 6¾ in (26.9 x 16.8 cm), Paris, Louvre

136b LIVELY, PAINTERLY EXECUTION IN A BAROQUE DRAWING

Peter Paul Rubens (1577-1640), Horse's head.

Black, red and white chalk, Vienna, Albertina

b

a

Section 8.4
Drawing the head as a whole

The unfathomable psychological aspect when facing an anthropoid ape positively demands color as a vehicle for mood. The head of a male bearded orangutan (fig. 138) gazes from the secret depths of his eyes, cast into shadow by the jutting eyebrows. The light, blueish purple of the forehead is encircled by a red halo of short head hair. The whole middle part of the face sinks into inscrutable darkness with the bright dome of the upper lip emerging from it, enclosed by the round, rust-red frame of the beard.

It is perfectly possible that quite different ways of using experience will emerge from these briefly stated principles as the artist's work develops a life of its own. The ways in which artists can identify subjectively with their object are as many and varied as the personalities of artists.

137 THE USE OF REALISTICALLY CONVINCING PAINTERLY MEANS

Unlike classical Renaissance art, the Impressionist approach does not find artistic beauty in form, but in suggestion of mobile living appearance, using such means as areas left blank. This drawing derives liveliness and credibility from the suggestiveness of its controlled jottings.
Adolf Menzel (1815-1905), Two views of the head of Emanuel, a saddle horse. Study for an unexecuted picture of a parade, 1873.
Pencil, 8 x 5 in (20.4 x 12.5 cm), Berlin, Nationalgalerie

138 ESSENTIAL UNITY OF OBSERVED FACTS AND PERSONAL EXPERIENCE (MALE ORANGUTAN)

A life study only conveying the bare facts will become wooden and dull if it is not supported by sympathetic feeling and poetic interpretation.
Gottfried Bammes (b. 1920), Head of a contemplative orangutan, 1984.
Watercolor on yellowish Ingres paper, 13 x 18¾ in (32.4 x 48 cm)

9.

Coming to terms with the whole animal figure

139 ANIMAL FORMS DRAWN AS BUILT DESIGNS

A study conceived as a constructed drawing requires us to bring together all we have learnt about anatomy in a total design concept, concentrating primarily on the structure of the body framework and including movement. This provides the basis for visualizing and imaginative power.

Drawing animals is not simply a question of fitting component parts together: we attach much more importance to layout and design – with their great potential for turning the experience of seeing, stored visual knowledge, discovery into something visible to others – than to representation. By 'design' we mean turning an idea into a picture, working from a creative idea or discovery and using a variety of media, irrespective of whether they are handled patiently and thoughtfully or quickly and spontaneously.

a) Typical figure of a herbivore (horse)

9.1
Drawings as built designs

The following are the main principles to be adopted in the pursuit of built design (fig. 139):

- The creation of order among masses and forms, assigning them their correct optical weight, in conjunction with the visualization of simplified forms. Construction of a hierarchy of forms (assigning values to forms).
- Developing a structural interplay between firm framework shapes and soft, variable muscle shapes.
- Bringing out the interaction of factors relating to proportion, construction, structure and dynamics.
- The integration of essential form as discovered in the animals treated here as representative.

The above principles have often been repeated in this book, but it must be remembered that 'built designs' are far from being the ultimate objective of our studies. On the contrary, they are a departure point for the appearance of individual and subjective components of artistic creativity, for the ability to visualize, imaginative power, intuition and inspiration. It is only from the starting point of drawings solid in construction and design that the way is truly open for us to call on the figure seen by our inner eye, the free-floating inner picture, the traces of which we capture in the sketch from imagination, the quick study of movement, or in free experiment with different means and media. We thus cross the boundary between what is concretely based to lapidary, free abbreviation. We move between these two poles: between the solidity of what is known through and through in practical terms, and freedom of expression and secure shorthand. Because trivia are absent, inner pictures derived from visual experiences often have great density of essence. Our memory has sifted out chance aspects that were not memorable by forgetting them. A course book such as this can only put forward principles to be followed and stimulate the student to work creatively. The truly artistic creative act cannot be taught.

b) Typical figure of a herbivore (cow)

9.2
Sketching

Sketching can be a planning stage, an independent activity or a training exercise. The essence of sketching is not speed – quickly jotting down in a few lines – but sureness of touch and an ascetic economy of means, often used to capture just a single aspect of the essential form. Of course the circumstances in which a sketch is executed influence the chosen approach and the lavishness of the means. There is a difference between conjuring up the massive repose of a standing bull (fig. 140), with powerful contours that require the outline to contribute greatly to the achievement of expression, using heavy hatching and a few smears of paint to convey the volume of the body; following the performance of a horse in the circus arena, trotting on the lunge (fig. 142) or rearing (fig. 53), drawing in pencil as if galvanized; and sketching a sniffing dog (fig. 141), with its tense back and neck, its moving tail and thin legs.

These few examples serve to demonstrate that sketching is not synonymous with speed, and certainly not with imprecision, carelessness or aimless freedom. A vague, haphazard approach, jotting down a snippet of what has been seen here, there and everywhere, comes from uncertainty as to the objective. Sketching with a knowledge of one's objective needs sureness of touch and engenders it. It also produces something that is complete in itself, and not just a scrap. When we look at figs 53 and 142 we should not wonder if the artist would have finished the sketches if he had had more time. With singular preciseness he has sketched just one single impression in an extremely concentrated form, with dynamism, expression of movement and just a hint at the circus background. The frantic lines are jotted down working almost blind, without looking down.

In this book life study has predominated, but in time you can be free of this, provided you have practiced looking with total intentness and have a valuable store of intensely felt events and visual experiences. This is where European and Asian approaches come close to one another: Chinese Buddhist art

c) Typical figure of a carnivore (dog)

and Japanese Zen art (fig. 143) rest on inner perception. A work of art has to open up suddenly like a mystic illumination, it must arise like a flash of lightning from the depths of the unconscious. That is why means are whittled down to a minimum – nothing to do with being in a hurry; a few brush strokes are enough to follow the innermost traces of the soul.

In his Indian ink drawing of a horse Sesshu lifted his brush only twelve times, and the animal stopping abruptly in its tracks is there (fig. 143b). The same is true of Hokusai's Galloping horse which has pictorial symbolism and poetic terseness. And it is surely right to point to the spiritual kinship of the American artist Sklar who characterizes a raccoon (fig. 146) from the tip of its nose to the toes of its back paws in a single curving line.

d) Typical figure of a carnivore (lion)

9.3
Free play

The call made on our inner resources in drawing means that it is more than just a hobby. But one of the forms it can take is free play. 'Human beings can only play if they are human in the full sense of the word, and are only wholly human when they play' (Schiller).

Free play means joy in practicing what we are fully conversant with. Doubts and worries which can sometimes be burdensome retreat. We are free to discover, invent and experience, open to daring, experiment and chance. Play attempts free creativity, observes the rules of the game, is a creative force. We are not talking about purely mental acrobatics, but making and doing and the freedom that comes with them, using various materials and media. Materials that are easy to handle are eminently well suited to our purpose, and working with them will suggest new ideas.

Our program for play may consist of:
- switching from close study to working freely (fig. 47);
- playing with pure line (figs 63, 113);
- a dialogue between the line and the mark (fig. 144);
- a dialogue between line and texture (fig. 147**b**);
- turning a mark into a form (figs 148, 149).

140 ASSESSING WHAT CAN BE DONE IN A LIMITED TIME
The artist must to some extent anticipate from the animal's behavior how long the model is likely to stand without moving, and decide what means to use for the sketch. For this drawing it was obviously possible to enhance the quick outline with texture, producing an impression of self-contained power.
Wilhelm Rudolph (1889-1982), Bull.
Pencil, smudged, 10 x 14 in (25.4 x 36.3 cm)

141 DRAWING WITH A BRUSH – A QUICK METHOD OF WORKING

There is a limit to what a quick sketch can contain. What is expressed here is the act of sniffing. A small flat brush filled with diluted Indian ink makes it possible to work quickly, presenting the image in broad lines, with powerful contours and virtually no breaks.

Diluted Indian ink and bristle brush on A4-size paper

142 INFLUENCE OF A TIME LIMIT ON THE MEANS USED

The tempo of movement and the changing scenes before him force the artist to record at great speed and with extremely limited means. The seeming cursoriness is in fact extreme concentration on the expression of movement. Small dimensions are appropriate for notes of this kind.

Josef Hegenbarth (1884-1962), Sketches of a circus scene. **Pencil**

a

b

143 JAPANESE ZEN ART

Shorthand symbols denoting natural phenomena are not entirely in keeping with European ideas of study from nature. These lines drawn with a brush in next to no time result from deep insight into the essence of animal life. They have nothing to do with speed per se and are the opposite of tense; they come from inspiration.

a) Sesshu (1420-1506), Horse. **Indian ink drawing, Nagoya Tokugawa, Japan**

b) Katsushika Hokusai (1760-1849), Galloping horse (from Mangwa). **Indian ink and brush**

144 A PARTNERSHIP OF LINE AND MARK

On its own, line carries on a monolog; combined with the patch, a dialog. The contrapuntal, highly contrasted play between the two is unmistakable: the broad patches make the line appear narrower, and the line reinforces the broad effect of the patches.
The author, Bear at ease, 1894.
Drawing pen and watercolor brush and diluted Indian ink on A3-size paper

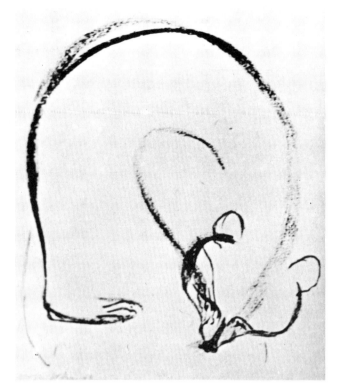

145 OPEN DETAIL – SURENESS OF EXPRESSIVE TOUCH

Brush marks, silhouettes and the directions of the limbs are the main expressive elements used to convey form in this free play with means. Work such as this could not be produced without lifelong familiarity with the daring but cruel sport of bull-fighting.

Pablo Picasso (1881-1973), Attack on a bull, 1957. **Brush and Indian ink**

146 A LITTLE SAYS A LOT

The sweeping curve from the tip of the nose to the back foot and a few minimal lines (so surely placed!) for the head create an unmistakable animal form, akin in its economy to the spiritual attitude underlying Zen art.

George Sklar (b. 1905), Raccoon, 1947. **Brush drawing, 10½ x 9½ in (27.4 x 24.1 cm), Philadelphia Museum of Art**

147 PLAY BETWEEN LINE AND TEXTURE

The fact that lines drawn in ink on paper sprayed with water run a little creates a relationship between them and independently drawn textural structures. Here chance effects are welcome.

a) The author, Bear at rest, 1984.
Pen and Indian ink on A3-size green-colored paper sprayed with water

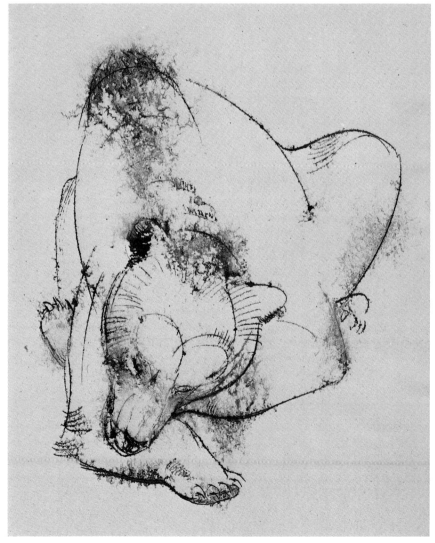

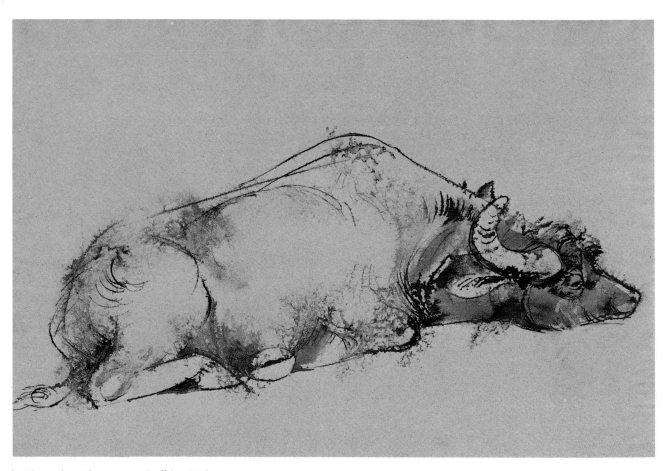

b) The author, Sleepy water buffalo, 1984.
Pen and Indian ink on A3-size brown-colored paper sprayed with water

Pure line is a track, a moving progression, and its rises and falls reflect hope and despair. If it entirely encompasses the form by returning to the starting point it creates an inside and an outside that are unambiguously defined.

The playful forms magically evoked by a few strokes in Picasso's bull-fighting scene (fig. 145) are not the outcome of a one-off flying visit to the arena, but an outpouring of lifelong visual observations and experiences, like the free play with line and patch (fig. 144) that suffice to express the comfortable well-being of a bear. While the mark stretches and spreads, the line moves constantly toward its goal. Marks can be arranged without any connection, but in their dialog with the line they are assigned a place.

Hatching and marks as internal shapes can suggest texture. The interplay of line and texture can be attractive if the line does not always progress with needle-sharp fineness, but trickles and runs, thus bringing happy accident into the game (fig. 147). Both playfulness and tension would disappear if the mark were simply used to fill in the contours of the figure. So the way in which marks are arranged and amassed, their size and the distance between them are part of the free play.

Collage (fig. 148) is also a suitable medium for this approach: unlike fluid watercolor, it does not force us to hurry. We can create textures that combine to produce form.

Just as the line and the mark or line and texture can carry on a game, the mark itself can run to give a form. If all we put down on paper are marks that run, the tension provided by articulation will be lacking, so here and there we carefully confine the flow, bringing in a little detail. A definite form eventually evolves from the mutual enhancement and completion (fig. 149). If we then include the variations available with color the graphic possibilities are endless.

The progression followed in this book from practical information to practical study, on to work from visualization and imagination and finally to free play, is based on my experience. Freedom comes at the end of a long process of preparation, not depending on fashion but growing and maturing as our artistic ideas develop.

148 PLAYFUL COLLAGE EFFECTS
The massiveness of the bull was first established with a broad brush outline of the contours and main forms. All sorts of offcuts of transparent self-adhesive foil in two different colors were then used to introduce textural effects into the outline. The author, Bull, 1984.
Wide flat paintbrush and diluted Indian ink, offcuts of colored self-adhesive foil on A4-size paper

149 DARING ELABORATION OF THE RANDOM MARK
The mark working on its own from pure chance can very well be used to evoke texture and form.
To avoid losing formal articulation and reduce the risk of the mark taking on a meaning of its own, all that is needed are often only a few carefully placed hard edges defining form.
The author, Donkey, 1984.